THIS BOOK is to
commemorate the issuance of the
official Kalispel medal

October 15, 1973

and is limited to 15,000 copies

No. **LIBRARY**

Louis Andraus

Photograph by John I. Griffin

JAN SAM, A SPRITELY SEVEN-YEAR OLD, symbolizes the Kalispel future. The tribe invests heavily in scholarships for its students to prepare them to compete successfully in an increasingly techno-logical society.

THE

KALISPEL

PEOPLE

by Robert C. Carriker

Scientific Editor: Henry F. Dobyns
General Editor: John I. Griffin

PUBLISHED BY INDIAN TRIBAL SERIES / PHOENIX

The author gratefully acknowledges the aid and encouragement of Father Wilfred P. Schoneberg, S.J., Archivist of the Jesuit Oregon Province, in the completion of this book.

Library of Congress Catalog Number 73-91579

PRINTED IN THE UNITED STATES OF AMERICA — Imperial Lithographers

MASSELOW, KALISPEL CHIEF, photographed in 1910 by E. Curtis.

CHIEF MASSELOW OF THE KALISPEL
1826 – 1920

THIS BOOK, the first on the Kalispel people, is dedicated to Masselow, chief of his tribe from 1887 to 1912.

Masselow's lifetime spanned nearly the entire pre-modern period of Kalispel History. Born the son of a sub-chief in 1826, his youth was spent in the forest and lake country of a region only rarely touched by white men. As a young man Masselow knew the first Jesuit missionaries to visit his people in the 1840's, and in 1853 witnessed the election of his father, Victor, as chief of the entire tribe. In succeeding years Masselow was groomed by his father in the ways of the Kalispel culture. He was also privy to his father's tribulations with gold seekers, railroads and government men who desired the cession of Kalispel lands.

Upon Victor's retirement in 1887 Masselow ascended to the chieftainship of the Kalispel people. The next quarter-century was the most critical in the history of that tribe. In quick succession the government pressured the Kalispel to remove from the Pend Oreille Valley, the tribe split and white encroachments reached intolerable proportions. Steady in his actions, peaceful in his intentions, Masselow held his declining and beseiged tribe together until his retirement in 1912, just two years before the Kalispel received a reservation.

Photograph by Robert C. Carriker

MR. LOUIS ANDREWS, Chairman, Kalispel Tribe of Indians.

WHEN THE KALISPEL INDIANS saw David Thompson for the first time, he was exactly what they expected. He was blond, medium-height, agile in appearance — and white. Several times in recent months the Kalispel had heard of white men who came alone or in small parties to the vicinity of Lake Pend Oreille in present-day north Idaho. Lewis and Clark passed to the south of the Kalispel three years earlier, and such important news traveled fast among the Interior Salish tribes. The official government expedition was followed almost immediately by less famous but equally inquisitive bands of commercial fur hunters and the Kalispel received reports on them, too. Now they saw for themselves. Their isolation was broken.

Though he was the first white man to visit the Kalispels, Thompson likely found the process of getting acquainted tedious for he had experienced it many times before in his lengthy career as map maker, trader and explorer for the North West Company. It was September of 1809 and Thompson was visiting "Kullyspell Lake" in one of several joint trading and reconnoitering assignments to this area. The initial contact was not extended: each party had his say, a brief barter took place, and then the Kalispels melted into the close-knit forest surrounding the lake to report the event to their summer camp not far away. From that day forward, in varying degrees, the Kalispels would be concerned with the ever increasing numbers of white men coming to the Inland Empire of the Pacific Northwest.

In the wake of Thompson came other fur hunters. Numerous American companies vied with the experienced North West Company and powerful Hudson's Bay Company from Great Britain in a multi-faceted competition. In succeeding years a few adventurers from each nation found their way into Kalispel territory but none chose to make it a regular route, partly because the Pend Oreille River, mainstream of the Kalispel country, flowed north and away from, it seemed, the mighty Columbia, central river to all trade activity in the Northwest. The Kalispel, unlike some of their neighbors to the east, did nothing to entice the fur gatherers for they could see no special advantage in courting

2

their favor. They lived as they pleased and found no fault with that. The respect they offered the mountain men was all they asked in return. Without encouragement the white contact diminished and for the next thirty years, until 1841, the Kalispel returned to their splendid isolation.

TRADITIONAL WAY OF LIFE

The Kalispel belonged to the family of tribes known as the Interior Salish, of which the Flathead tribe is generally accepted as the most prominent member. Also included in the clique are the Spokane, Coeur d' Alene, Pend Oreille and various smaller bands. Closely allied with the Flathead by custom, language, appearance and character, the Kalispel originally lived in the Montana plains just east of the Rocky Mountains. About 1700 Blackfeet war parties began to move south and west against the Flathead group and the Kalispel were gently pushed, in several migrations, across the Rockies.

Exactly when in the early eighteenth century the Kalispel settled into the Pend Oreille Valley and its surrounding region is only a speculation by scholars. Kalispel tradition says only that when their forefathers were coming from lands beyond the Rockies the people halted at present-day Priest Lake while scouts were sent to seek a suitable village site. In their travels the scouts ascended a mountain and peered down

3

upon what seemed to be a shimmering, blue lake. Descending they learned the sea of blue was not a lake, but immense fields of camas in bloom. (Lewis and Clark noted a similar experience at a different spot on their journey through the Northwest!) The plant was edible; nearby flowed a fish-rich river, and game abounded in the mountains. Upon the scouts' recommendation, this valley was selected as headquarters of the Kalispel nation.

The Kalispel roamed a country of great diversity, spectacular beauty and almost unmatched bounty. The tribe ranged widely over lands below the forty-ninth parallel (United States — Canadian boundary) east as far as Mount Spokane in Washington, south to Lake Pend Oreille in Idaho and west to the Clark's Fork River of Montana. Nomadic by nature, the Kalispel laced with trails this land of great forests, clear, rushing streams and crisp, blue, deep lakes. It has been estimated the tribe roamed an area over four million acres in breadth.

In summer the tribe scattered over the countryside living off the abundance of nature and forming only temporary camps with mat tipis woven from available tule, rushes or cattail. These mats could easily be rolled up and taken from one camping spot to another. Wide strips of bark were available in this land of thirty foot circular trees, and could be placed horizontally

4

LUCY PEUSE stands in a "tule weed" house made from reeds and mud found on the
Pend Oreille River. This photograph taken at the turn of the century shows a very
ancient form of Kalispel home then used mostly as a drying and smoking house and
general workshop.

to serve as a temporary shelter. During winter the tribe ordinarily settled along a nine mile length on both shores of the Pend Oreille River about forty miles north of its source at the lake of the same name. Perhaps as many as one thousand tribesmen formed three or four villages in the sheltered river valley known for its abundance of camp supplies.

Socially and politically the Kalispel were unpretentious and democratic. There were several bands within the tribe, each with a chief and sub-chief, though none was privileged or superior to others. The central authority in the tribe was possessed by one head chief who resided in the headquarters village on the middle Pend Oreille River. All the chiefs formed a council where large affairs of the tribe were aired. Camp life was informal, though there were strict regulations regarding fires, sanitation, guards, position of lodges and herding of horses.

Some men had two or more wives, but after the smallpox epidemic of 1800 drastically reduced the tribal membership this was less true than before that date. As other illnesses took a toll of the Kalispel intermarriage with surrounding tribes increased. A Kalispel girl became eligible for marriage following a simple puberty rite devised by her grandmother. The maiden would spend six to eight days alone in the woods, eating nothing and praying profusely. Upon her return she was recognized as a woman.

Young men reached manhood in a longer, more detailed custom. Beginning as early as five the boy's father began purposely misplacing some personal article or his medicine bag at a nearby spot. The son was sent to retrieve it, the hope being he would profit from this communion with adult medicine articles. As he grew older the length of such exercises increased and the spirit within the articles spoke to him. Finally, at age thirteen or so the boy was sent into the mountains alone to find his medicine. It might be an object, an animal or an event that appeared in reality or vision, but from this the boy would learn his worth and his future. From that day forward he would always carry a portion of his medicine with him, be it a feather, fur, hoof, rock or leaf.

Death was met indifferently by the Kalispel because they had no concept of good or evil in an afterlife. The person's spirit, they thought, was merely transported away from the body in a north and then westerly direction, just like the river on which they lived. Prior to the coming of missionaries the Kalispel were said to even bury alive the very old or the helpless young. This practice was modified with the introduction of Christianity, of course, but as late as 1912 Spokane newspapers carried the story of the death of an aged woman in the tribe who refused food or water for fifteen days choosing to die in a variation of the ancient ritual.

Corpses were dressed in clothes donated by relatives and then placed in a shallow grave and covered with stones. If the tribe was in strange or uncertain territory no stones were used and all traces of the burial were obliterated for fear of the grave being disturbed by enemies or thieves. Other than the presentation of favorite articles in which to dress the deceased, the only other tribute paid to the dead was to place gifts in the grave or, in the case of a man, to kill his horses.

Among the Kalispel there was no Great Spirit, not even a word to identify such an idea. All good or bad luck emanated from an unseen old woman or sorceress. Accordingly, the Kalispel were great believers in charms. Medicine, however, was almost always a personal matter for there were few shamans.

Dancing among the Flatheads usually centered about war, but because the Kalispel were a peaceful tribe these ceremonies had little use in their camps. Today the tribe still enjoys a festive war dance, but it is chosen more because of the exciting name than because it has a significant part in their heritage. Likely the most meaningful Kalispel dances were those held before and after the hunt. Bodies swayed in dim campfire light, songs pierced the air and supplication to spirits was interspersed with individual men chanting their own medicine songs or narrating a vision of tribal success.

Winter in the northern climes is neither unanticipated nor unprepared for. The dozen or more summer camps along the lakes and rivers of the region contracted into a few villages when a nip hit the air and signs of fall became clear. Strong lodges were engineered at the winter camp, some dug underground with side entrances. Others were merely earth-covered huts. Most family dwellings were conical tipis constructed of mats rather than hides, with a twenty-two pole black pine foundation. Two related families inhabited each lodge, though some were big enough for three. There was an entrance at each end of the lodge, with separate fire and smoke holes for each family. Winter camps usually also had a single long lodge for common ceremonies, dancing and guests.

While women worked on the camp in late fall, men spent their final snow-free days stockpiling food. In a short time cold blasts, with temperatures dipping sometimes twenty to thirty degrees below zero, would freeze shut fishing holes and clog trails with snow crusty enough to cut a horse's leg. A final deer drive was organized — at times netting upwards of three hundred animals — and all berries and fish possible were preserved.

Encampments made in December were not disbanded until March. During the time of winter camps household utensils were fashioned. Slivers of flint were chipped into knives, kettles were sculptured and split cedar-root baskets were woven. In addition, clothing was repaired and new items of apparel tailored. Because they crossed the Rockies to hunt buffalo only infrequently, the Kalispel had few outside garments from that beast. Instead, rabbit-skin robes were pieced together for use as coats. Skin ponchos from deer hides were less worthy substitutes. Deer skin formed the bulk of both men's and women's regular clothes from shirts to leggings to moccasins. A good part of all the energy spent in making these clothes involved fringing, trimming and ornamenting intricate and individualistic designs.

Tension was eased among tribesmen held captive in the grip of long, and sometimes brutal, winters by storytellers. The tribe had a chief storyteller, aided by story men in each of the bands. In their mythology the Kalispel were like all other Interior Salish tribes and revered the coyote as their cultural hero. Assuming human characteristics to deal with the beaver, wolf, lynx and other animals, this animal was the most frequent vehicle to explain to the tribe such great events as the origin of the sun and moon, the emergence of monsters, and numerous moral lessons. After the coming of the missionary Biblical stories such as creation, Noah's Ark and Lot's wife became intertwined in the folklore of the tribe.

One favorite tale among the Kalispel concerned a turtle with fifteen brothers "as alike as so many berries" who challenged a frog to a spirited overland race. The slow witted frog never detected that he was racing sixteen turtles strategically placed around the course and so lost a humiliating race plus the wager of his tail. Hastily renouncing land travel, the frog entered the lake to forever hide his shame.

In spring the Kalispels came alive with an energy that corresponded to the awakening of the country in which they lived. Rivers freed themselves from their icy restraints, streams gushed forth pregnant with life and mountains grudgingly released their enormous snowpack. The tribesmen separated into smaller bands, each headed by a chief or sub-chief, and set out for nearby hunting, fishing and rooting grounds. In this way an undeterminable number of camps were established. Inasmuch as there was no specialization among the Kalispel, several camps could be in search of the same game or berries.

Infrequently in the spring some Kalispel would cross the mountains to the west and visit the Colville tribe for purposes of salmon fishing, for none of these fish entered their own waters. More likely than not the privilege would be repaid in June when the Colvilles would visit the Kalispel near the main village outside present-day Cusick, Washington, and together the two tribes would dig the camas root from the

11

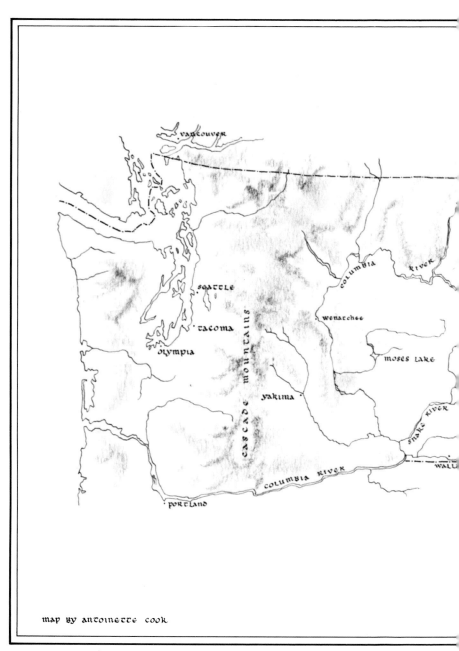

Within the map:

VANCOUVER

COLUMBIA RIVER

SEATTLE

wenatchee

TACOMA

MOSES LAKE

OLYMPIA

CASCADE MOUNTAINS

YAKIMA

SNAKE RIVER

COLUMBIA RIVER

WALL

PORTLAND

map by antoinette cook

MAP 1. The Pacific Northwest and Aboriginal Kalispel Territory.

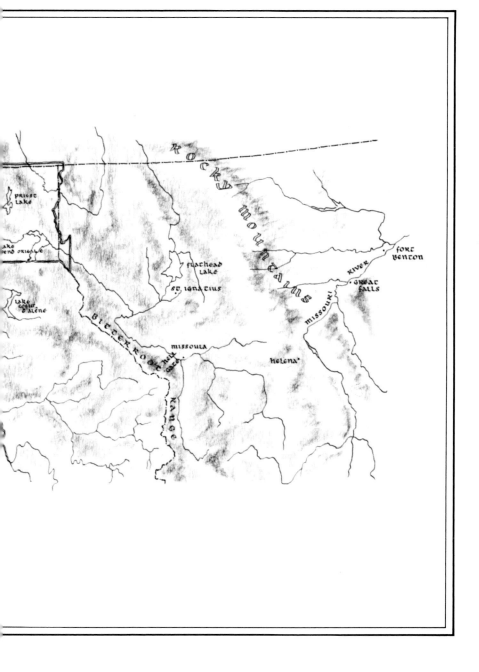

prairie nearby.

Though bands of the Kalispel spread out in April and May, a large number were certain to return to the vicinity of the main village during camas time. The camas is a small, white, onion-appearing root removed from the earth by means of special long, crooked sticks. After the tribe had gathered all they cared to acquire the cooking began. Into a hole about a foot deep the roots were placed with a covering of stones. A fire was ignited on these stones and later a layer of wet grass or hay was placed on the hot pavement. Another row of camas was then placed, more wet hay and finally a bark overlay and more stones upon which a fire was burned for up to seventy hours. The camas, when so cooked, becomes black and sweet. It can be made into nutritious loaves, is a treat boiled with meat or can be dried and preserved for long periods. So proficient were the Kalispel at this, and so abundantly did the root grow in their lands, that many tribes knew the Kalispel as "Camas People."

After the camas festival the Kalispel bands returned to the forests and streams. The deer was the most easily hunted animal by virtue of its great numbers in the region, but cougar, elk and bear were also popular targets. Some locations, of course, were better suited for one specie of game so if the band determined to have that animal it adjusted its location accordingly.

14

Water fowl, for example, was expecially plentiful on the Pend Oreille River near the main winter camp. So numerous were ducks and swans that it was impossible to sleep on those nights when the birds were restless or easily spooked. Likewise, Priest Lake was noted for an abundance of mountain goats and beaver.

While the Kalispel had no claim to salmon fishing points, they nevertheless had access to a large number of other game fish sites. Some bands followed the whitefish migration to Priest Lake using giant weirs — interlaced branches placed across a stream to direct the fish to only one opening — while others used basket traps, spears or the simple hook and line method for a vide variety of trout.

Fishing was made more pleasurable to the Kalispel when they took to their low riding, sixteen foot canoes. As some tribes, like the Nez Perce and Comanche for instance, were widely known for their horsemanship, the Kalispel were reputed for their use of the canoe. The Flathead, who had no canoes and used only rafts, called the Kalispel "Paddlers" as an accolade for their proficiency with the bark craft. Kalispel canoes were easily the finest in the Northwest, being of swift and light white pine with ribs from cedar and carefully selected black pine roots used for sewing. Of the same general shape as other Salishan canoes, those of the Kalispel differed slightly in their end design for their vessels had

15

THE JOYOUS KALISPEL USE OF A DISTINCTIVE CANOE for fishing and river trans
portation may be inferred from this 1910 Edward Curtis photograph of canoes or

the Pend Oreille River in front of the Kalispel village.

distinctive cut-off and turned-down snouts. Some scholars testify that this uniqueness may be traced to an Iroquoian influence, for the Iroquois were often employed as aids by the North West Company fur traders. The Kalispel themselves attest that such a design is but a simple precaution against the gusty winds encountered on the broad, flat Lake Pend Oreille.

Because water was the natural highway for the Kalispel they were not known among other tribes for their use of horses. This is not to say they had none. Thompson in fact, confided in his journal that the Kalispel "are abundantly provided with horses."

Acquiring their first horse was considered an event of note by the Kalispel. According to folklore some people saw horse tracks in the sand and were mystified. They called others but none could identify the prints. Then, near the river bank they observed an Indian on his horse and he seemed to be quite at ease. They watched him enter the river and swim across on the horse and when he came near they gathered around and examined the beast with much curiosity. Because they had no word for horse in their vocabulary he was given the same term as for a dog. Later, when horses became more numerous a related word was coined for them alone.

Beautiful and bountiful as their land was the Kalispel seldom had visitors and almost never an adversary. The Colvilles, Spokanes and Coeur

18

d' Alenes were neighbors, not trespassers. When invited they did come to the Kalispel lands to dig camas, but otherwise they respected ancient boundaries. Lake Pend Oreille was a central trading point for several tribes, beginning with David Thompson's establishment of Kullyspell House on the northeast shores in 1809, but the traffic did not encroach on those areas heavily settled by Kalispel bands in summer or winter. The great trade route between east and west, both before and after the advent of horses, was the Pend Oreille River. This easy passage through the mountains left Lake Pend Oreille near Sandpoint, then followed downstream to a point between Newport and Usk where a land trail or traverse went more directly to the Colville tribe. The headquarters village of the Kalispel was not on this traditional Indian trade trail.

Positioned on the interior of the Salish family of tribes the Kalispel fought few wars. All around them were friends: to the north were the Lower Kutenai, the Colville were on the west, the Pend Oreille to the east and the Spokane and Coeur d' Alene to the south. Once or twice the Kalispel engaged the Coeur d' Alene or Lower Kutenai in an intramural battle, but these flare-ups lacked lasting animosity. The Blackfeet were, perhaps, the only traditional enemies of the Kalispel and the series of wars that nation initiated with the Salish tribes only once reached

19

into Kalispel country. It is thought that prior to 1820 a war party of Blackfeet raiders came to Sandpoint where they recklessly attacked a summer camp of Kalispel. The Kalispels responded with ferocity, drove off the invaders, and inflicted several casualties with no loss to themselves. Father Pierre De Smet, S.J., an early traveler in this region confided to his diary in 1845 that "It is a common saying in the mountains that in battle One Flathead or Kalispel is worth five of his enemies."

The Kalispel, then, were unchanged by the brief appearance in 1809 of a few fur hunters. In succeeding years the fur trade continued unabated, yet unnoticed by the Kalispel. That the Kalispel do not record in their folklore any significant meetings with whites during these years does not mean there were no important visitors to their wild mountains and lakes. One caller in 1841 was Sir George Simpson, Governor General of the Hudson's Bay Company, in the midst of a round the world voyage that included stops at Company posts. Traveling west across the Rockies, Simpson and his party reached Lake Pend Oreille ("Kullespelem Lake") at six one evening just in time to witness "a beautiful sheet of water, embosomed in mountains, to which the burning woods, more particularly at night, gave the appearance of volcanoes." The next morning the small group of officials portaged the falls of the Pend Oreille

River later known as Albeni Falls and there encountered, but did not intrude upon, some two hundred or more Kalispels preparing to journey toward Montana's plains in search of buffalo.

THE MISSIONARY PERIOD

One white man to have a profound influence over the Kalispel was Father Pierre-Jean De Smet, S.J., missionary extraordinary. Father De Smet was, when he met the Kalispel, just one year into a career of spreading the gospel, exploring and peace-making among Northwest tribes that would consume his talents and energies over the next thirty-three years.

In November of 1841 De Smet had just completed his pastoral work among the Flathead and was enroute to new duties with the Colville tribe. His route would normally have followed the Indian trade trail along the Pend Oreille River with a transfer to the winding mountain path that went to Fort Colville. On such a course De Smet would have left the Pend Oreille River before it flowed near the headquarters village of the Kalispel. Fate intervened in the form of two camps of Kalispel which De Smet came upon while passing west along the Clark's Fork River toward Lake Pend Oreille.

Stopping to chat with the tribesmen De Smet found them friendly and inquisitive. The priest was himself curious about this band for they spoke a dialect of the Flathead language, were similar to that tribe in appearance and manner, yet had only a rudimentary knowledge of the white man. Before he departed that camp De Smet baptised twenty-four persons.

Continuing his journey a few days more, De Smet arrived at Lake Pend Oreille. Poised on the threshold of Kalispel country, De Smet marveled at the natural beauty of the waters and woods. "We traversed a forest, which is certainly a wonder of its kind;" he wrote his superior, "there is probably nothing similar to it in America." Birch, elm and beech, usually small elsewhere, he found rivaling the cedar in size and resembling large candelabras majestically placed around a massive column. Continuing on three days more brought the weathered Jesuit to the Pend Oreille Traverse. Instead of going immediately toward Fort Colville as originally planned, De Smet now elected to continue down the Pend Oreille River toward the main village of the Kalispel.

In a few miles scattered Indian lodges began to appear. Quickly the number of camps multiplied. It was autumn and the Kalispel were drawing near their main village as winter's unmistakable signs manifested themselves. At last the main camp came into view. Beaching his canoe, De Smet was warmly received. Henceforth, in his correspondence the missionary

22

would call these indians, Kalispel of the Bay, in reference to the broad, bay-like expanse of sheltered river that lapped against the prairie upon which the village was laid.

De Smet paused but a few days among the Kalispel, yet found many promising attributes among the people. Little touched by outsiders, the Kalispel, thought De Smet, could well serve as lessons in humility for the Christians of Europe. One hundred and ninety tribesmen were converted to Christianity, including the chief who took the name Loyola. The priest was pleased with his work and knew he must return, perhaps the next time to found a mission.

In April of the following year De Smet did return to the Kalispel and what he saw warmed his apostolic heart. He was grateful to learn that the brief nights he had spent instructing the tribe in prayer the previous November had not been forgotten. The tribe assembled morning and evening to recite common prayers with "much fervor." In addition, the chiefs were "incessant in exhorting the people to the practice of every good work." Sadly, the priest speculated, a great number more would seek baptism were it not for the plurality of wives and a fondness for gambling. As it was, sixty adults were converted. It would be some time before De Smet would return, but in the meantime a new missionary arrived among the tribe.

At De Smet's request Father Adrian Hoecken settled in as the resident priest for the Kalispel of the Bay. "The first thing," wrote Hoecken in a letter home, "which struck me on my arrival among them, was a truly brotherly love and perfect union, which animated the whole tribe and seemed to make them but one family." Hoecken quickly learned to work closely with the chiefs, for he found them the real fathers of their people. Sickness, want, marriage, regulation of hunting, fishing and distribution of the catch all were among the chief's responsibility. When Loyola promulgated approval of the new Blackrobe and promised whatever changes he deemed necessary to make, Hoecken knew he had found a fruitful vineyard of the Lord.

Continued residence with the Kalispel exposed for the first time to white men the many qualities of the tribesmen. Pride, it seemed, was absolutely foreign to the Kalispel. Humility and meekness were their virtues. Hoecken said he often witnessed grey-haired old men and even chiefs sit with ten and eleven year old children for hours at a time making patient explanations. Moreover, Hoecken added, "Complaints, murmurings and backbiting are here unknown; blasphemy has never been uttered by an Indian: there are not even words in his language to express it."

When De Smet revisited the Kalispel again in November of 1844, he was welcomed "amidst volleys of musketry and the sounding of trumpets." The Kalispel were growing in civilization, and, at the same time, Hoecken was enthusiastic about the tribe's ecclesiastical progress. With so many new converts a church was now in order and De Smet, in typically dramatic fashion, selected a beautiful grotto in the neighborhood of the main village which he named New Manresa in honor of the cavern outside Catalonia, Spain, where the Jesuit's founder, Ignatius Loyola, once spent a year in fast and penance. The New Manresa Caves remain today on the Kalispel Reservation and Catholic services are held there on special occasions.

De Smet moved on, a captive to a busy schedule, leaving Hoecken behind. During the long cold months that followed, Hoecken, now reinforced with another priest and two lay brothers, came to know his charges well. Suffering that winter was great among the 500 tribesmen. Even the most closely woven mat tipis were drafty and nearly the entire tribe suffered from chills. The partially underground lodges were somewhat warmer but improper ventilation caused campfire smoke to irritate the inhabitant's eyes, resulting in an alarming rate of blindness among young and old alike. Hunger was another serious problem. For decades the tribe concentrated their fall deer hunt in the low lying hills that flanked the main village. In time these herds were so decimated that the last

several year-end drives were exceedingly small. A
saturation kill could not be made in the same
locality year after year. The result of such poor
planning was that the kill this year had been low
and many people were starving. Hoecken con-
cluded that agriculture must be developed
among the tribe.

At midwinter Hoecken joined De Smet at
Albeni Falls, where another camp of Kalispels
were wintering, to concelebrate Christmas Mass.
That day in the Kalispel country was an event of
note. Two religious services plus a gala banquet
preceded a baptism of 124 new converts. The
most moving event for the priests occurred when
Catholic Indians, some of two years standing,
acted as godparents for others.

Back at the Bay of the Kalispel, Hoecken
joined with his assistants in laying plans for a
building and farming program among the
Kalispel. With proper leadership the industrious
tribe assembled a permanent settlement that
included fourteen log houses and a large barn in
just four months. In addition, some 300 acres
were sown in grain and villagers tended thirty
cows plus an assortment of hogs and chickens.
The livestock, of course, like the plows, spades,
scythes and carpenter's tools, had been brought
to the Kalispel on De Smet's previous trips. It
was De Smet's practice to have missionary
supplies sent from Europe to the Hudson's Bay

THIS KALISPEL PHOTOGRAPHED BY EDWARD CURTIS in 1910 wears a costume that any Kalispel male might well have donned during the preceeding century. With his hair braided, this man wears ear pendants of the general style that gave the Pend Oreilles their name, a chokertype necklace, and a trade blanket such as fur traders introduced to tribes in the Kalispel area early in the Nineteenth Century.

Company settlements on the Columbia River, then to pick them up when in the vicinity and walk or paddle them inland to the four missions he had established.

So elated was De Smet with the progress of his beloved Kalispel that he ordered the establishment of a formal church at the main village. A spot in the neighborhood of New Manresa was selected and De Smet himself felled the first tree for the Reduction soon to be called St. Ignatius Mission. So remarkable is the Kalispel achievement at this early date that this village on the Pend Oreille River may properly lay claim to being the oldest continually inhabited community in Eastern Washington.

The tribe De Smet left after the dedication of St. Ignatius Mission was a curious combination of western culture and ancient innocence. Experiencing little face to face contact with whites through 1841 the Kalispel retained a docility, honesty and love of labor that many other tribes of the region abandoned. Then, after more than thirty years in seclusion from the whites, missionary activity began with a flourish. Instead of retreating, the Kalispel welcomed the Blackrobes and accepted their western religion and culture. Receiving tools and seeds directly from Europe via the Columbia River, the Kalispel quickly demonstrated a facility for Euro-American technology. From that day to this the Kalispel would increase their knowledge of western society, make Catholicism an important part of their lives, and yet retain much of their old culture.

Mission life was, unfortunately, never as prosperous for the Kalispel as was hoped. Undermining nearly all the efforts of Hoecken and his assistants was the plain fact that De Smet had erred in the location of the mission on a flat plain near the river. Ordinary spring run-off overflowed the river to the steps of the church, and unusually high water threatened the existence of the village. Floods in the spring of 1845 and 1846 inundated the newly sown fields and it was not until the third year's attempt that a crop was actually harvested and put into storage for winter.

Those years when the Kalispel's farm was turned into a marsh were especially trying for Hoecken. He had promised much but could deliver little. Instead of potatoes, wheat and barley to supplement the winter diet, the tribe was reduced to "pine-moss cooked with a little *gamache* (gruel), a meal of which no beggar would care to taste." Hoecken was much loved by the Kalispel, though, and at his urging the tribe rallied to new efforts. With fresh ardor, fences were patched, crops resown and fields tilled.

In the spring of 1848 the Indians broke new grounds on the hillside east of the village, abandoning hope for their original garden. At

29

the new site the soil responded fairly well to cultivation and at least the first crop was successful. The regeneration of the mission seemed complete when more buildings were constructed including a kitchen, dining room, carpenter shop and stable. The mission church was also finished that spring and measured sixty-five by thirty-five feet in squared logs, with walls twenty feet high. Additionally, a residence was built for the Jesuit community, described by one of the inmates as "poor but not unbecoming."

Despite their increasing success as farmers and builders, the Kalispel grew restless. After five years it was clear to the tribe that the meadow on which they lived was only a few inches of loam on a clay base, and thus was not suited to long-term farming. Moreover, April and May were the only growing months for it was inevitable a flood would come in June. The only question was how severe it would be. Hoecken wrote his superior asking for permission to move the mission to another location in the Pend Oreille Valley. It was not only the hazardous spring that made the present location undesirable. The winters were also something to think about. The priest's letter was dated March 25 and there was yet ten feet of snow on the ground. The request was not immediately acted on, so for the time being the settlement remained unchanged.

While the Kalispel were students of technology and theology under the Jesuits great events were taking place elsewhere in the Pacific Northwest. Protestant missionaries like the Whitmans and Spaldings were evangelizing other tribes to the south, and, more importantly, organized a campaign to bring settlers to the Columbia River country. Emigrant traffic significantly increased on the Oregon Trail after 1846 when the Americans settled the boundary problems of the Oregon Country with British Canada. Then in a double dose of disaster the Whitman Mission near Walla Walla fell to angered Cayuse Indians in 1847 and the government responded with the first official declaration of war on any tribe of the Columbia Plateau. The war was short and undramatic but its shock waves reached clear to the Kalispel. It was unlikely the Kalispel with their peaceful nature would join a war of any kind. That they could avoid by choice. Of no choice to them, however, was the increased number of white settlers arriving in the Northwest. For the moment the Kalispel were tucked away in the far northeast corner of Washington Territory (created in 1853), out of the path and desire of the mounting numbers of pioneers.

After President Millard Fillmore signed the bill creating Washington Territory, he named Isaac I. Stevens Governor and Superintendent of Indian Affairs. An energetic and resourceful man,

31

Stevens determined to visit his Indian charges while enroute to Olympia, and concurrently accepted a position offered by the War Department to lead a railroad survey crew to Puget Sound.

Several Indian tribes were met by the Stevens party, though nothing decisive was agreed upon. After reaching the summit of the Rockies in the Flathead country Stevens divided his command. Dr. George Suckley joined one group taking the Clark Fork River to Lake Pend Oreille, then to continue west on the Pend Oreille River. Making good time in their canoes the surveyors were reluctant to leave them for a sixty mile horseback trip to Fort Colville when they arrived at the Traverse. For the first time in four decades someone became interested in following the Pend Oreille River downstream to an anticipated junction with the Columbia. Interestingly, the Kalispel offered the party neither encouragement nor information on such a course. Hesitant to proceed without some advance information, the government men placed in their report a notation that the reason they were stymied at this point was that the Kalispel, whose hunting grounds lay in the opposite direction, were "too indolent to travel for the sake of exploring or for pastime," and did not even know the character of the river on which they lived.

Spending one night at St. Ignatius Mission

before returning to the Traverse, Suckley found the Kalispel of great interest. Surprised to learn the mission was nearly nine years old, he quizzed Father Hoecken at length. This conversation when written up and brought to the attention of Stevens, ultimately became very important in Kalispel affairs.

As a man of science, Suckley carefully recorded Kalispel habits as he saw and learned of them. The church, he observed, lent a stability to the tribe for "its vicinity is looked upon as headquarters." Statues, brazen crosses and bronzed fonts, handwork of the Indians so cleverly crafted as to "lead one to suppose that they all must have been imported," adorned the handsomely carved and gilded alter. This labor, "rich, substantial and beautiful," was not the extent of the Indians deeds. A grindstone, hewn from native rock, tin-ware, a blacksmith's bellows, ploughshares and bricks were other accomplishments.

Aside from the dwellings, now increased to sixteen log houses, a blacksmith shop and storeroom, Suckley was most impressed with the 160 acre terraced farm tended by the Indians. Wheat, barley, onions, cabbage, parsnips, peas, beets, potatoes and carrots were the principal products of the soil. Carrots were by far the most popular vegetable. Small children, said Hoecken, "cannot, cannot resist the temptation" of snatching them from the garden.

33

Adults were equally fond of peas and cabbage, but "beets, and particularly onions, they dislike."

Like most other visitors to the Kalispel Suckley also remarked on the overwhelming beauty of the country, their unique canoes and the peculiar habit of annually exterminating deer herds in the final fall hunt. To meet bare subsistence levels during the winter the tribe needed about 800 deer. Having left none to breed in their rape of the region in past years, that prospect was dim for the future. Suckley hoped the tribe would develop a substantial agriculture before the deer ran completely out.

Whatever game was killed during the harsh winter months, Suckley understood, was distributed among the most needy families, irrespective of who the hunter may have been. This was a custom initiated by Chief Loyola and continued by his worthy successor Victor. Suckley found the present chief a "small man, young, and of good countenance; but so good and amiable is his disposition, that he is scarcely able to maintain his authority over the tribe." Whipping was Victor's most common punishment for a serious offense, but it was never decreed unless the culprit agreed it was a just sentence.

Hoecken had, by this time, written not less than six letters to his superiors requesting a change of location for the mission and he spoke of this to Suckley. New houses at another location were offered the Indians, but they would only reply, "This is our country; here are the graves of our forefathers; here we were born, and here we wish to die; we do not want to leave our country, poor as it is." Speaking himself to as many of the estimated 420 tribesmen as possible, Suckley found it "interesting and amusing to listen to the account of their plans, shifts, and turns, in overcoming obstacles, at their first attempts, their repeated failures and their final triumphs." Clearly, the tribe planned to make their future in the Pend Oreille Valley.

That the Suckley account properly identified the Kalispel of the Bay was significant. Using this information plus other inquiry, Stevens was able to draw a clear picture of tribal structure just west of the Rocky Mountains. Bordering the Flathead on the west was the tribe known as the Upper Pend Oreille, so called because "Pend Oreille" refers to "Hanging Ears" or "Ear-Drops", the practice of wearing shell earrings as noticed by early North West Company French traders. There was also a Lower Pend Oreille tribe, a separate cultural and geographical identity, though they seldom used the term Lower Pend Oreille themselves. These Indians only infrequently wore ear pendants and rather called themselves Kalispelem in reference to a great camas-digging place at Calispel Lake. The Kalispelem were actually composed of divisions:

the Lower Kalispel or Kalispel proper who headquartered at St. Ignatius Mission; the Upper Kalispel who ordinarily made camps around Lake Pend Oreille and the Pend Oreille River as far west as Newport; and the Chewelah, a small, semi-autonomous group in the mountains immediately west of St. Ignatius Mission.

All three divisions of the Lower Pend Oreille held lands in joint use and occupancy in spite of the fact they were politically separate.

GOVERNMENT INTEREST
IN THE KALISPEL

Shortly after arriving in Olympia, Governor Stevens prepared to investigate the Territory of Washington and, at the same time, treat with the Indians within his jurisdiction. From May through October of 1855 at Walla Walla, Hells Gate and Fort Benton, Stevens negotiated the cession of Yakima, Cayuse, Nez Perce, Blackfoot, Flathead, Upper Pend Oreille and Kootenai tribal lands plus their individual promises to move to designated reservations within a year. The Coeur d' Alene, Colville, Spokane and Kalispel tribes were scheduled next, in late October, when Stevens received word of the Yakima Uprising and dropped all plans for more councils so he could return to Olympia.

Of the four tribes with no treaty, the Kalispel were the most important to Stevens. The Upper Pend Oreille cession had been detailed at the

Hells Gate conference in July and the governor then hoped to shortly make a similar agreement with the Lower Pend Oreille, specifically the Kalispel. Stevens was especially anxious because he understood the Kalispel were already in Montana and on the Jocko Reservation assigned to the Flathead, Kutenai and Upper Pend Oreille tribes. To him there remained but a formalization of what was already fact. On October 26, 1855, Stevens instructed his agent with the Flathead, Dr. R. H. Lansdale, to contact the Kalispel and ask them to meet with him at Hells Gate. The meeting was hastily suspended two days later when Stevens learned of the Yakima trouble. He then asked Lansdale to make a new appointment with the Kalispel and conclude the treaty himself.

The source of Steven's misinformation lay in the removal of St. Ignatius Mission in 1854 to the Flathead Lake area. Recurring floods, the poor quality of soil near the village on the bay, and the harsh winters were all factors in the decision by Father Hoecken to move the Reduction. Sometime during the spring Victor joined with Chief Alexander of the Upper Kalispel and together they searched for a new location. None was found in the Kalispel country, most probably because Hoecken required the new site to be central to more tribes than just the Lower and Upper Kalispel. At last the selection was made in a verdant valley of the Upper Pend Oreille tribe called Sinielemen, a rendezvous for many tribes in years gone by.

During August and September nearly all of the Lower Kalispel joined with the Upper Kalispel in a move to the new mission. Five small barges were readied to carry the yield of the final harvest and pack horses were secured for the human cargo. Doubtless the Kalispel were puzzled that a village worked so diligently for ten years, so rich in wood, water, game and berries, and so close to the hearts of firm Catholic Indians should be uprooted. At one point the tribe halted and said "el tam" — not any more. The priests stepped forward however and told them not to act like children, they must come. All but two or three families did.

Thus it was that Stevens heard that the Kalispel were already on the Jacko Reservation when he completed the Hells Gate Treaty in July of 1855. What Stevens did not know was that before he could return in October, the Lower Kalispel returned to their homeland on the Pend Oreille River.

Painful as it was to leave their beloved Father Hoecken, the Kalispel felt uncomfortable with the multiplicity of tribes that swelled to over one thousand the population of the new mission. Chief Victor declared, "we found that we could not keep our autonomy." Not all Kalispel returned to the ancient holdings on the

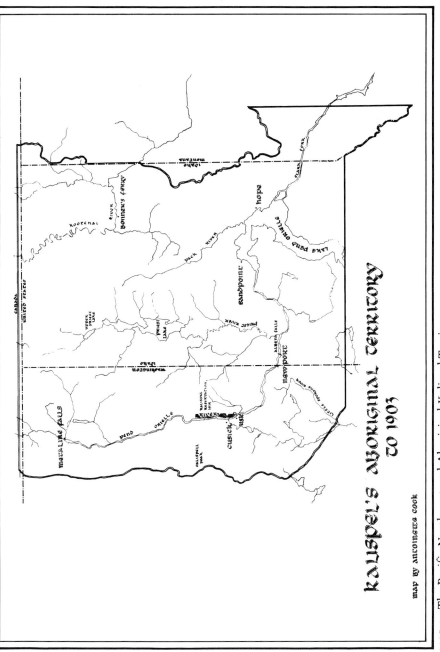

MAP 1. The Pacific Northwest and Aboriginal Kalispel Territory.

Pend Oreille River for the Upper Kalispel remained in Montana. Yet those Lower Kalispel who did once more cross the Rockies held forever more the sovereignty of the Kalispel name and lands.

Life back at the bay was never the same without Hoecken and the other Jesuits. In far too short a time many in the tribe, testified Victor, were "in a miserable condition drinking, gambling and all the vices following it." Correspondingly, farm lands decayed and the log buildings became dilapidated from misuse and neglect. With these thoughts heavy on his mind, Victor agreed to meet Lansdale in March of 1856 to consider the treaty proposed by Stevens.

Dr. Lansdale dutifully explained to Victor the treaty provisions. In return for a cession of all Kalispel lands in Washington Territory, and removal of the tribe to the Jocko Reservation of the Confederated Tribes (Flathead, Kutenai and Upper Pend Oreille), the government promised to provide $40,000 over a twenty year period to aid in the tribe's adjustment to a new location. Assignment to the Jocko Reservation, and consequently the new St. Ignatius Mission, was not totally unacceptable to Victor in light of the recent debasement of his tribe. Cession of all Kalispel lands was. A compromise was suggested by Victor and his brother Simon whereby the Kalispel would move to the Flathead Reservation, yet keep possession of certain lands on the Pend Oreille River, roughly half the proposed cession, giving up all others. The Pend Oreille preserve would be, according to Simon, "a small spot to return to in safety," if the tribe were harassed by enemies in Montana. Lansdale could not agree to such a proposal for he was only the agent of Stevens and was not empowered to make or delete articles. Victor refused to budge from his position and Lansdale, after a private talk, could only dissolve the council. The general pattern of Kalispel history for the next half-century was drawn. The Kalispel would never waver in their demand for a reservation — even a small one — within traditional holdings.

In Olympia, Stevens hoped the Kalispel would change their mind. His door was open to further talks, but at the moment he was tied up in the Yakima War. Kalispel affairs would just have to wait. Presently the Yakima War expanded and by 1858 the Coeur d' Alenes and Spokanes were asking the Kalispel to join them at the war circle. The Spokanes and Coeur d' Alenes suffered from the same malady that incited the Yakima — trespassing gold seekers — but they had an additional complaint against the government in that they had no treaty whatsoever ceding lands or designating a protective reservation. In this they had common ground with the Kalispels and therefore sought their association.

On the other hand the Kalispel were not seeking a quarrel with the whites. They rejected the overture, though it is estimated some two-score Kalispel with family ties to the Spokane did join the hostile camp. The fires of war continued to burn brightly and a second time the Kalispel were courted. The Kalispel called a great council and debated the invitation for several days. Hotbloods strung their curved bows and held a war-dance, but few joined. In the end only about twenty-five Kalispels moved to the Spokane-Coeur d' Alene war party. Ironically, the first warrior killed in the opening skirmish to test this consortium was a Kalispel.

With soldiers sallying back and forth to the south of the Kalispel camps many tribesmen felt it was unsafe to remain in the Pend Oreille Valley. Accordingly, the tribe divided into bands and made extended expeditions to fish in British Columbia or hunt buffalo in Montana. Some parties were absent as long as two years. When they returned the war was over, the Spokanes and Coeur d Alenes had their treaty, but no reservation, and more whites than ever were present in the region. As a result of their official non-participation in the war and the recent sojourns away from their homegrounds, the Kalispel found themselves in 1860 the forgotten, non-treaty tribe of the Northwest.

GOLD MINERS, RAILROADS
AND FARMERS

In the first fifty years following David Thompson's reconnaissance on Lake Pend Oreille, the Kalispel country was relatively free of white men. Most who came departed quickly: the fur traders, the Stevens expedition, even the busy missionary. After St. Ignatius Mission was moved to Montana, Father De Smet had few occasions to look in on his Indians on the bay. In 1859 he did return to the Pend Oreille River country, this time at the request of the Federal Government as an emissary of goodwill to the recently subdued Northwest tribes. The priestly ambassador found "generosity, docility, the love of labor, great courage and piety are (still) among the characteristics of this tribe. . . ." Little known to De Smet all of these attributes were about to be seriously tested by three new groups of white men just beginning to slash their way through the Kalispel forests — gold miners, railroad surveyors and dirt farmers.

Trails abounded in the Kalispel country. Paths worn smooth by moccasined feet criss-crossed the mountains leading from lake to stream, stream to prairie. Where foot traffic did not lead, the watery highways did. For all its vastness, the Kalispel land was easily traversed. During the Colville gold panic of the mid-1850's the Kalispel were little troubled with visitors. Only slightly more annoying was the low-yield strike of 1860 on the Pend Oreille River below Metaline Falls, north of the main Kalispel villages. The discovery of gold on Wild Horse Creek in British Columbia late in 1863, however, was an event that brought hundreds of prospectors and businessmen to the Kalispel lands.

Wild Horse Creek, in the Canadian Kootenai country, was directly above the unceded lands of the Kalispel and the only routes through were Indian trails. Uninvited miners hustled along the Kalispel paths. Individuals could be tolerated, but shortly whole caravans began to monopolize the trails, or even break new ones. No one seemed to remember the Kalispel had no treaty with the government, they had made no cessions of land. Fortunately this predicament never came to a violent summit for the traffic was significantly reduced in 1865 when an east-west route was blazed through British Columbia.

Included in the residue that remained from the human waves that passed through the Kalispel lands was Bonner's Ferry. Established for obvious purposes on the Kootenai River of northern Idaho, this settlement lay in the center of Kalispel lands. Apparently the newly convened Territorial Legislature of Idaho (1863) did not recognize Kalispel property then they authorized this colony, and again later when they approved use of Kalispel trails for a pack-train outfit commuting from Walla Walla to Wild Horse via Bonner's Ferry. At the same time California interests supplying the gold fields of the same period in Helena and Virginia City, Montana, boldly cut horizontal routes across the Indian property. Remarkably, the Kalispel suffered these indignities in peace. No hand was raised against the whites.

Meantime, the village on the bay slowly raised itself from ten years of fallowness. A decade after Victor's gallant decision to stay on traditional lands, the Kalispel were once more herding cattle, breeding horses and cultivating a garden that surrendered, in 1867, 200 bushels of oats, 650 bushels of potatoes, and ten tons of hay. Such progress soon came to the attention of the Indian Agents at Fort Colville and the Flathead (Jocko) Reservation who reported it to the Commissioner of Indian Affairs. It was not long before a clerk in Washington, D. C. was summoned to review the Kalispel's status. When he returned empty-handed from the files a new series of events was set in motion once again to acquire Kalispel lands.

A final check in the Bureau of Indian Affairs showed that the Kalispel were only one of nine tribes in the Washington Territory-Idaho Territory region without a reservation. Settlement of this situation required a special committee so, following Executive Orders of April 9 and July 2, 1872, the Shanks Commission was duly authorized. Regretably, the Commission's efforts were little more than a replay of the Lansdale affair. Just as Lansdale was bound to the treaty written by Stevens, so too the Shanks Commission had the power only to sign tribes to a pre-arranged reservation; they could not amend the original stipulations.

Personal observation of the bureaucratically devised reservation quickly convinced the Shanks Commission members that the pre-arranged proposal was unworkable. For one thing such culturally diverse tribes as the Spokane, Colville, Kalispel, Okanogan, Methows and San Poil would all be bunched together. In addition, evidence uncovered by the commissioners suggested the whole idea for removal was forced by interested whites who would greatly benefit from the release of new sections of lands. Another drawback was that the location of the government sponsored reserve, west of the Columbia River, was unacceptable to eastern tribes. Even if it were, Shanks estimated, it would take many thousands of dollars to relocate and establish the tribes. The Commissioners, in response, devised an alternate, rectangular shaped reservation along the Washington-Idaho border. Washington officialdom, however, failed to act on this recommendation and shortly the whole matter was dropped.

Unaffected by inconclusive government gyrations the Kalispel remained in their villages on both sides of the Pend Oreille River near the former site of St. Ignatius Mission. Hunting and fishing continued to be the chief food source of the 400 residents of the Bay of Kalispel, though farming continued to spread. Timothy hay now extended some fifteen miles up both sides of the river and vegetable gardens continued apace.

Though the Jesuits came less often after the relocation of St. Ignatius Mission it in no way reflected a lack of interst in the Kalispel among the community. The main problem was in schooling missionaries in the Kalispel tongue. The Kalispel language was very similar to that of the Flathead, and there were priests who knew the tongue. Unfortunately the Montana tribe was much larger than the Kalispel so these men seldom were able to break away to the Pend Oreille River. One remedy to the problem was to teach more Jesuits the language and in pursuit of that goal three Jesuit scholars completed in 1879, after more than thirty years work, a three volume dictionary of the Kalispel language in more than one thousand pages. Bound in wallpaper or other scrap paper, this dictionary, of which no more than one hundred copies were printed, remains today, by virtue of its age, subject and size, one of the rarest volumes in the study of Indian languages.

As studied by the Jesuits the Kalispel language was characterized by a gutteral "g", a harshly pronounced "k", and an absence of consonants such as "b", "r", "d", and "f". The dialect's form was surprisingly simple with no exceptions to verb rules and almost no plural irregularities. Like those who spoke the tongue the language was remarkable in its conciseness and exactness of phraseology. You could not misunderstand for there was not one word which admitted of two meanings.

Father A. Diomedi was one Jesuit who occasionally visited the Kalispel between 1868 and 1878 and left in his letters a vivid description of a tribe he capsulized as "converted but not yet civilized." Victor, still a prominent figure, was now in his declining years as chief of the tribe. Diomedi found him "the very picture of laziness and dirt." The priest felt that the chief was not adequately leading his people and as a result the tribe's governmental system had broken down. During the summer of 1877, for example, the son of a sub- chief, avenging his wife's honor, murdered another man and Victor shrank from any action for fear of recriminations. Family bonds correspondingly became stronger as the tribal government became more lax with no resident priest or other outside authority to provide external sanction.

The village itself, as Diomedi found it, was nothing more than a conglomeration of vermin-infested huts perched on the lower ridge of hills fronting the Pend Oreille River. Agricultural progress notwithstanding, the Kalispel seemed

48

less civilized than before the first missionaries arrived. Gambling was decidedly their worst passion bringing distress among families and being the cause for stealing and quarreling. Cards were one form of gambling, but among the men the most addictive wager was the stick game. Crowded in a single long lodge the Indians arranged themselves in a circle and begin to sing familiar tunes. When the prelude was over one of the gamblers took two small sticks, about one-fourth of an inch thick and two inches long, one of which had a long thread attached, and held them, one in each fist, in such a way as to show the thread passing through the fingers of both hands. The others must then guess in which hand is the stick to which the thread is connected. Excitement reached a high pitch before guessing began, and singing and yelling went on for several minutes before anyone would venture a guess. The man who guessed correctly gained one point and lost one if wrong, and when the number agreed upon was reached the game was over.

For all their shortcomings, Diomedi nevertheless loved the Kalispel for their innocence. Relatively untouched by the white man the Kalispel's life was simple, even primitive, in its daily performance. A day in the Kalispel camp usually began at dawn when a blue smoke issuing from the lodges indicated the night's rest was over. Victor rang a handbell calling the tribe to morning prayer in his lodge after which all returned to their own tents for breakfast. The men spent the day hunting, young boys tended the herds and the women busied themselves sewing, washing and tanning skins. "What I admire in that tribe," wrote Diomedi, "is their docility and respect, as well as the sincerity of their faith, which they have preserved constantly from the beginning."

Diomedi, in his semi-annual visits to the tribe, several times witnessed the Kalispel's deer roundup in the fall. The Indians prepared for this crucial event by a solemn ceremony of burning all moccasins. When the moccasins were half destroyed by fire they were taken out of the fire and distributed among the hunters. In the morning the Indians dispersed along a piece of country seven or eight miles in diameter carefully hanging pieces of the charred leather in a pre-arranged pattern along known deer trails. The deer were then driven into traps or ambushes, the animal actually following the Indians' plan because of his natural reaction to the heavy smell of humans left in the old footwear so strategically placed.

The Kalispel continued their secluded life for less than a decade after Diomedi's last visit. In the normal progress of the westward movement white settlers reached the boundaries of the Kalispel country by the middle years of the

THE WIFE OF CHIEF MASSELOW, photographed in 1910 by Edward Curtis. Her attire suggests that Kalispel women adopted European style clothing more rapidly than did their husbands. The preaching of Roman Catholic missionaries and the urging of civil authorities in the pre-reservation period of Kalispel life undoubtedly hastened female donning of dresses.

1880's. Gold seekers of the 1860's has been modest in number and only passed through the Kalispel lands. The new influx of whites was more numerous and had permanent settlements in mind. Colville feared that eventually a war would errupt over the "unextinguished" Indian title to a rich area increasingly coveted by whites. In Montana the Flathead agent's primary concern was the restlessness caused by the Kalispel who were reported "sneering" at those tribes who had signed treaties, only to see many of the promises unfulfilled. Moreover, it seemed unfair that 400 Kalispels should retain their vast hunting and fishing preserves while larges tribes were crowded on remote reserves. The Kalispel were several times interviewed by Special Agents and each time insisted they would not leave their own lands for a reservation elsewhere.

In the nation's capital the Kalispel were an all but unknown comodity. The 1870's and early 1880's belonged to the Cheyenne, Sioux, Nez Perce and Apache wars. Civil and military authorities gave scant attention to the un-threatening Kalispel, isolated in an area of little settlement.

Nearly thirty years after Victor's refusal to relinquish aboriginal lands for a reservation in Montana the Kalispel were living the same life as their fathers, free and independent, on the Pend Oreille River. There had been some minor conflicts with gold seekers, trespassing pack trains and over-eager ferry operators at a few spots, but these were more portents of the future than actual events of strife. For the most part the Kalispel enjoyed the advantage of being elusive, non-treaty, reservationless Indians. Then one morning the piercing whistle of a Northern Pacific Railroad locomotive shattered the silence. It was as if a signal had been sounded for a race throughout the Kalispel lands to be run by farmers, timber cutters and town builders.

Economic necessity required the Northern Pacific to bring pioneers to the northwest. So they came in a steady stream to settle, cut and build on unceded lands. They cared not for vague arguments from the Kalispel about ancient title to the lands. To them a homestead act or a bill of sale from the Northern Pacific was all they needed to know. In a twinkling, the advantage became a liability: the Kalispel were naked before the law, for they had no treaty and no reserved property.

The instrument that demonstrated this defenselessness was the Northern Pacific Railroad. Chartered by Congress in 1864 with almost the same privileges as the Central Pacific and Union Pacific railroads, the Northern Pacific was charged with building a railway across nearly two thousand miles of wilderness from Lake Superior to the Puget Sound.

The Northern Pacific entered aboriginal Kalispel lands in 1879 but survey and track crews moving northward from Walla Walla were busy along the edges of Lake Pend Oreille and did not actually interfere with the tribe's villages. For two years, or until the 225 miles from the Columbia to Lake Pend Oreille were spanned, each month brought more workers, more surveys, more towns.

A railroad was crucial to the growth and economy of northern Idaho and eastern Washington. Essential to the railroad was its land grant. Without it the costs of construction were prohibitive. One of the reasons the Northern Pacific raced to lay track seventy-five miles around Lake Pend Oreille in 1881 was so it could qualify for its grant of 1.9 million acres in Idaho. This land, in turn, was saleable for operating cash and in the next six years the corporation disposed of some seven and one-half thousand acres for $26,323. Prices ranged from $2.60 an acre to $4 on credit. Timber land and lakefront property was predictably costlier.

By 1884 the trickle of settlement became a constant pressure on the Kalispel. Incredibly patient with the encroaching whites thus far, the Kalispel were now besieged on even the Pend Oreille River. Action of some kind by the tribe was mandatory. At first settlers were frightened, warned and released. This remedy proved insufficient when, in time-worn Western tradition, the whites returned, the next time heavily armed.

Chief Victor was in a quandry. None of his tribe desired war. So peaceful, in fact, were the intentions of the Kalispel that not even all of the tribesmen advocated remaining on the Pend Oreille River lands. Some of the tribe felt it was better to remove to the Colville or Flathead reservations and avoid completely the impending violence. Yet, this was not what Victor had held out for since he first rejected the government's offer of cession twenty-eight years before. Since 1856 Victor had demanded that the Kalispel would cede their ancient title not for money but for a reservation of their own choosing on the Pend Oreille River. In an effort to save the unity of his tribe, and, at the same time avoid bloodshed, Victor, in company with other chiefs, journeyed west over the mountains to visit Agent Sidney Waters on the Colville Reservation.

Sidney Waters was a consciencious and concerned Indian agent. The Kalispel were among his assigned charges, but he seldom was able to meet with them as Colville affairs monopolized his time. On many occasions he had requested a settlement of the Kalispel land question by the Commissioner of Indian Affairs, but none was ever forthcoming. With the specter of violence hanging in the air, Waters met with Victor, chief of the "wildest Indians attached to this Agency."

In the course of their discussion, Waters came

to realize that the Kalispel meant to hold their lands no matter what pressures were brought to bear. Victor, proud of his tribe's agricultural achievements, emphasized their domestic stability. Yet, he explained, hunting and fishing were mainstays of Kalispel subsistence. They must not lose their traditional hunting and fishing stands. Victor was a reasonable man and suggested a settlement, one that belied his years of seclusion on the Pend Oreille River.

Victor accepted the fact that the whites were not going to leave the lands they already occupied. It was merely academic to argue the justice of that case. What the Kalispel hoped to avoid was a ballooning white settlement in the Pend Oreille Valley which would eventually suffocate the tribe. Such was the deplorable situation of their neighbors the Spokanes. Victor moved that the government simply allow the Kalispel to select their own reservation and then receive payment for any other lands relinquished. If the government declined to reimburse the Kalispel for those lands already taken without permission, Victor proposed that an alternate form of compensation might be to allow each Kalispel head of a household to select a 160 acre allotment outside the reservation.

Waters agreed to promote such an option with the Commissioner of Indian Affairs when the Kalispel, in turn, promised not to harass the whites on their lands. It was so agreed, signs of friendship and trust were exchanged between the two parties and Waters posed one final question to Victor: why did he not send Kalispel children to the government school? Because, came the answer, "I did not want them to learn the language of their enemies." With that Victor and his breechcloth-and-blanket entourage faced the rising sun for a full day's ride over the Chewelah's mountains.

Waters was true to his word. To him a bond given was a bond kept. So sincere, in fact, was Waters that even after he was replaced in 1885 as Indian agent at Colville, he continued to bombard the Bureau of Affairs with urgent pleas for action in the Kalispel crisis. It is wrong, he emphasized, for the Kalispel lands to be generally classified as unsurveyed public domain. On that basis individual farmers were beginning to homestead the Pend Oreille Valley. The situation was critical, and perhaps combustible. Whites, he testified, are extremely aggressive with the Indians, especially for someone squatting on as yet unopened lands.

The warnings of Waters fell on deaf ears. The Bureau of Indian Affairs was busy with other events and could not give immediate attention to a non-violent tribe. As will sometimes happen in a bureauocracy, while the Bureau of Indian Affairs was content to hold the line on Kalispel affairs, the General Land Office aggravated the situation by surveying the Kalispel lands on the

Pend Oreille River. The Kalispel knew that where the government surveyor trod, the settler could not be far behind.

Meantime a new Colville agent tried to familiarize himself with the Kalispel problem. In his report of August, 1885, he determined the Kalispel's traditional hunting lands were, indeed, infringed upon by the whites, but the tribe was as yet relatively undisturbed on the old St. Ignatius Mission site. Echoing a sentiment made many times before, the new agent felt the Kalispel should be removed to the Coeur d' Alene or Flathead reservations or allowed a regular land allotment at the General Land Office. He did not specifically ask for a Kalispel reservation.

Simple as the solution seemed to be, the Bureau of Indian Affairs lacked both the energy and the inclination to close the case. With the land survey completed in 1886 pressure from the whites became intense. The Kalispel who in 1884 tried manfully to avoid trouble were two years later ambushing settlers and frightening them off. Rumors reverberated across the mountains of murders by both sides, though physical evidence of foulplay by either side was never produced. In the spring a unit of cavalry from Fort Sherman, Idaho Territory, moved to the vicinity.

The Colville Agent urged in his annual summary that "something be done to either place the Indians upon a reserve or compel them to take up their lands in severalty, for sooner or later serious trouble might arise, as the whites are determined to settle in the Kalispel Valley, and the Indians are as determined not to permit them."

THE NORTHWEST INDIAN COMMISSION

It took time, but at last a decision was made in Washington, D. C. to empower another commission to deal with the Kalispel and all other non-reservation tribes of the Inland Northwest. There is speculation that the agent's pleas were less effective in the capital city than those of the War Department which was now drawn into the fray when troops from both Fort Sherman and Fort Spokane were placed on alert in response to hearsay of Indian treachery in the secluded Kalispel mountains. In any case, a commission consisting of Congressman John V. Wright, Dr. James W. Daniels and Mr. Henry W. Andrews was formed to reduce the number of reservations in the Northwest and to settle on reservations all of the scattered bands of non-reservation tribes, not the least of whom were the Kalispel.

Representing the Kalispel at the opening session of the Northwest Indian Commission on April 21, 1887, at Sandpoint were chiefs Victor, Masselow, Nicola and Michael. They were supported by an estimated 150 tribesmen, including some thirty-one men who attended one or all of the council sessions. Masselow was now the chief of the Kalispel, Victor having resigned this position in favor of his son just prior to the Sandpoint conference. Michael was Masselow's sub-chief.

It was obvious from the outset that the government intended the Kalispel to become a reservation tribe, but not on their own lands. The task before the assemblage was to reduce the number of reservations, not create new ones. The Kalispel were asked to accept a place on the Flathead Reservation and Victor absolutely rejected this idea. He then rose to defend this decision and his policy of the previous thirty-two years.

Represented by Nicola, an orator of great repute, Victor pleaded for understanding. His people were hunters and fishers, they needed great mountains, wide rivers and lush prairies. His people were peaceful, they had never killed a white in anger. They had lived for many generations in the Pend Oreille Valley. It was a place they would not leave. Victor then described Kalispel territory to the commissioners, making it clear that the Kalispel were willing to sell part of their "country" but not their "lands" on the Pend Oreille: "We are now talking about our country, not our land. Our land is not for sale."

Masselow made only a brief presentation. He expressed love for his domain, saying the Great Spirit had made their country and given it to them. The new chief further stated that he found no objection to the commissioner's terms, but that it would be "criminal" for his tribe to give up their lands and move elsewhere. Nicola next expressed fears to the council that if the tribe refused to remove the government would in some way punish them. Michael, dressed unlike the others in the white-man's suit and accessories, had little to say publicly. It was known, however, he favored the proposal.

The commissioners, for their part, were reluctantly unyielding. They were directed by their superiors to reduce reservations in general, and place the Kalispel on the Flathead or Coeur d' Alene reservation in specific. They simply could not bargain on the basis of a separate Kalispel reservation. At best the commission could only offer lands on the Flathead Reservation plus $37,865 to be expended for resettlement costs.

Surprisingly, one Kalispel stepped forward to place his mark in the government document. Michael, claiming to represent the majority of the Kalispel present, came to terms. The Kalispel were bound to be soon dispossessed from the Pend Oreille homelands, he felt, so it was best to accept lands on the Flathead Reservation now, rather than someday be forced onto the less desirable Coeur d' Alene Reservation. Michael's headmen, Pierre, Bighead, Joseph and Antoine also assented to the treaty. Masselow withheld his signature and unceremoniously decamped from Sandpoint with his father and most of the tribesmen still in attendance.

With Michael's approval assured, Wright was anxious to meet again with Masselow. He was even more desirous when the council's interpreter stepped forth with information that Masselow was personally inclined toward the arrangement but could not betray his father's wishes. Wright sought out Masselow — pictured by the commissioner as "attached to the wild roving life which his band leads" — but when located at the village he denied such a statement. He further said "that he would not go to the Flathead Agency unless the Great Father took him there by force." To Masselow the crux of the Sandpoint meeting had been a desire by the commission for the Kalispel "to leave their country for a short time so the whites might take it."

Under the circumstances the Northwest Indian Commission treaty of April, 1887, was never submitted to Congress and consequently went unratified by the United States. Without Masselow's signature the document was useless. Discouraged, the commissioners returned to the capital. They had done their best to protect non-reservation Indians from white contact. They were pleased the Spokane, Kootenai and several others had responded favorably. Yet among the Kalispel only sixty-odd tribesmen accepted shelter on the Flathead Reservation. The remainder of the tribe was now to await alone, without government aid or protection, the fate of the growing white settlement.

A DECADE OF INTENSE WHITE SETTLEMENT

The year following the Sandpoint council brought renewed white trespass. Weakened by the loss of the sixty-three persons who went with Michael, the tribe was now even less capable of effective resistance than before. Illness competed with desertion to diminish the ranks of the tribe and by 1890 the population of the Kalispel hovered around one hundred and twenty-five souls. In consideration of the fact that only a decade before the tribe numbered over 400 individuals, it was a drastic reduction. Huddled in their receding village the Kalispel scarcely knew, or cared, that in 1889 Washington became a state and the following year Idaho shed her territorial status.

Already staggered by the after effects of the passing of the Northern Pacific, the Kalispel suddenly found themselves squeezed by yet another railroad. This time it was James J. Hill's Great Northern. Survey work between Spokane and Bonner's Ferry began in the spring of 1890.

Fortunately for the Kalispel the Great Northern was not a land grant railroad, so no Idaho or Washington deeds were given. Still, the Great Northern was a public carrier, and to be profitable it needed public riders and shippers. It therefore became a promoter, if not seller, of Inland Empire property. The Kalispel situation sounded even more hopeless when, with the General Land Office survey now complete, the Pend Oreille Valley, or Calispel Valley as whites liked to call it, was officially opened to settlement in 1890.

Up to 1890 Pend Oreille County, Washington, traditional village site for the Kalispel, was only sparsely occupied by whites. The first homesteaders seem to have laid their claims in 1884, and two years later the first store in the region was opened near the site of the old St. Ignatius Mission at Usk. After returning from the Sandpoint meeting the Kalispel abandoned their property on the west side of the Pend Oreille River, concentrating their reduced numbers on the eastern shores. Shortly it became problematical how much more the Kalispel could draw into themselves. The Great Northern track bed was completed in 1892 and all around homesteads sprouted. Newport was the site of a dozen claimants by that time, and Priest River in Idaho was similar.

As if the railroads had not done enough to encourage settlement in northern Idaho and

AS LATE AS 1910, when Edward Curtis photographed this quiet Kalispel camp scene, these native Americans clung tenaciously to their traditional life-way.

BY 1940, when Father Edward Griva S.J. photographed part of the Kalispel village, these Indians had been forced to the bottom of regional economy and society.

eastern Washington, an 1885 lead-boom at Metaline Falls, to the north of the Kalispel, promoted foot and water traffic along the Pend Oreille River. The *Bertha, Torpedo* and *Dora* regularly plied the waters from Newport to Ione only four years after the strike. Naturally, increased business activity brought mail service.

A non-stop parade of letters from Colville agents to the Commissioner of Indian Affairs about the Kalispel continued through the last decade of the century. The Bureau of Indian Affairs remained uncracked.

Mere words could not stop the white tide of settlement any more than they could attract the attention of the Commissioner of Indian Affairs. Settlers continued to pour into the Pend Oreille Valley, staking claim to obviously Indian land. Easily some of the best property along the Pend Oreille River was that occupied by the Kalispel across the river from Cusick and Usk. Avaricious settlers naturally zeroed in on those lands. Constant harassment followed. Chief Masselow was, for example, once arrested on trumped up charges of burglary. A favorite technique of whites was to get a foot on Indian land by leasing. After paying rent a year or two they filed on the farms with no mention to the land agent of a prior arrangement. Captain John W. Bubb, new agent at Colville, wrote in 1894 that "a determined effort is being made by the whites to freeze them out and the Indians do

66

not understand the situation."

If the whites could not be thwarted at the point of conflict Agent Bubb hoped to close off their confirmation. The Land Office in Spokane was asked to refuse filings on Indian land. Though this seemed a worthy solution to a thorny problem, it had loopholes. First there was no authorization by the General Land Office and secondly, there was no way for a clerk in Spokane to know what property near Usk and Cusick was already inhabited by Indians. Bubb later learned that the Spokane land agent fully knew which were Indian lands, but never refused a white man's claim. This led Bubb to believe, as he told his superiors, that a hearing on such land claims would mostly result in defaults by the whites "as they told me, they knew it was Indian country, but as things were going they would file and take their chances."

Remarkably, the Commissioner of Indian Affairs responded to Bubb's plea. Instructions to take a population census of the Kalispel and make a survey of their lands was forwarded to the agent. In the course of this assignment Bubb learned of the death of Victor. Chief from 1853 to 1887, Victor more than any other man personified the Kalispel. As the spokesman for his tribe in three different councils, Victor had remained firm, but not inflexible, in his requirement of a separate Kalispel reservation. Even at the time of his death, Victor declined to compromise his principles. The aged sage called his people together and told them he desired to be buried near the traditional village and he wanted, likewise, all his people to remain on the east side of the river and be buried there, too.

By 1895 the survey was made, the census taken and the Spokane Land Office ordered not to accept white land claims in the known vicinity of the Indian village. Those whites already holding Indian lands were not challenged. All was ready for the official allotting of lands. Such action was delayed time after time for one reason or another. Bubb saw that without allotments the Kalispel were still incapable of legal defense against the whites and took it upon himself to bring a number of Kalispel men to Spokane where he personally entered a homestead claim in their name.

Holding the line on white settlement while filing claims for some Indians was certainly not the close of Kalispel land problems. They still had no reservation or special allotment, and, perhaps most dangerous of all, nothing had ever been done to disallow the great acreage granted the Northern Pacific. By the close of the 1890's this problem pushed to the fore yet another irony of the Kalispel case. The Kalispel were willing to acknowledge the presence of the Northern Pacific even to recognizing their near two million acre grant in eastern Washington and northern Idaho. To do otherwise would be

68

unrealistic. What bothered the Kalispel was that the very land on which they were now settled was considered part of the Northern Pacific land grant and *they* were in trespass on railroad property. Oddly, the Kalispel could not be properly alloted by the federal government because each alternate section of land belonged to the Northern Pacific.

Up to this point, the moral justness of the Kalispel cause was never a factor in any decision made, but times were changing. Beginning with the Dawes Act, America awoke to the cruelties of her Indian policy. Proded by frightful statistics of Indian attrition, removals and injustices, the American conscience arose. Books were written, legislation prepared, conferences held and organizations chartered, all with the hope that the moral justice of the Indian's cause might be coordinated within the American legal structure.

The Interior Department quickly sided with the Kalispel against the Northern Pacific. Clearly, the 1864 charter to the railroad stated that lieu lands could be substituted for primary lands. A simple trade, however, was not possible. The "lieu land" question was a political hot potato at this time in Washington State. In the first place the Northern Pacific was not always quick to designate its lands under the grant. When pressed for cash the company selected only as much land as it needed to sell, but hedged on the other areas because then once designated they would have been subject to property taxes. The settlers, meantime, grew impatient and filed their claims. Later the railway might choose that section and evict the farmer. In 1888, Guilford Miller contested these actions and his case dragged through the courts during the nineties. Finally he won the right to stay on his claim and the railroad was told to select lieu lands. The decision said that persons on odd-numbered sections prior to 1885 had valid title to their lands. Clearly the Kalispel had been on their lands as long and the Attorney General was so informed.

The Assistant Attorney General for the Interior Department took the case under advisement and gave his opinion that "even if the railroad company should relinquish the lands now occupied by the Kalispel Indians existing law could not permit the company to select lieu lands for those." And there the matter lay for nearly another decade.

In the interim the world passed into the Twentieth Century. The United States elected Teddy Roosevelt President, and in 1903 the Kalispel were transferred to a new agency at Fort Spokane. The agent at Fort Spokane was Captain John Webster, an Army officer on temporary duty. Webster began reading all reports filed by the previous agents, especially those of fellow Army officer, Bubb. He noted that a survey had been run, but allotments were not made, save the individual claims Bubb filed for certain Kalispel.

Webster was especially interested in the Assistant Attorney General's decision in the question over railroad lands. For one thing, he noticed that overlooked legislation altered the Kalispel controversy. Not all settlers had been satisfied with the Miller case, especially the fact that it revolved around the single date of 1885, so Congress stepped in, under pressure, and passed a law in July of 1898 which permitted the Northern Pacific to relinquish, in lieu of other sections, lands which had been "purchased from the United States or settled upon or claimed in good faith by any qualified settler." This was a loophole for the Kalispel.

Traveling to the Kalispel village in the summer of 1905, Webster learned his was the first visit by an agent in ten years. Energetically Webster talked to the approximately one hundred tribesmen and attended a council. His resulting report was frank and to the point. He found that "from the points of view of the utilitarian the Kalispels may be of no service to the community or may even be a useless incumberance." Yet they are self-supporting and "inoffensive." All of their past troubles, he said, are the result of the "selfish greed of a few white settlers." It was his decision, then, to urge the Department of Interior to clear the title to the odd-numbered

71

railroad sections for "in absolute justice the title belongs solely to the Kalispels. . . In the interest of humanity and justice some way should be provided whereby these Kalispel Indians may be permitted to retain at least a small part of the lands justly their own in the beautiful valley to which they are bound by the most sacred ties, and where, in the language of one of their leading men, they 'wish to remain with their good name.' "

The pleasant result of Webster's persistence in the railroad land matter was that in 1906 the General Land Office permitted the Northern Pacific to take 2,500 acres in alternate lands for those on which the Kalispel were settled. The Kalispel were deemed in posession of the lands in question on August 30, 1881, the day the railroad was definitely located and the rights of the company to a grant attached.

The Kalispel lands were now free of any Northern Pacific claim. Previously, in 1895, white settlement on Indian lands had been halted and Agent Bubb had surveyed a possible alloting area. All that remained, the final step in an incredible lengthy journey to justice, was for the allotment to be made.

THE STRUGGLE FOR ALLOTMENTS

Though the Kalispel had generally peaceful, if not cordial, relations with the settlers surrounding them, some greedy whites resented any allotment for the Kalispel. Attempts to dispossess the tribesmen on grounds of their detrimental effect on the so-called civilized community of the region had begun prior to the 1887 Northwest Indian Commission talks. At that time the Kalispel were widely accused of murders and war scares. None, of course, were ever substantiated. In the twenty years following that episode more subtle methods of incriminating the Kalispel were devised. Led by a greedy would-be land baron named Napoleon La Clerc, a group of citizens at Newport insisted the Kalispel were guilty of setting forest fires, general lawlessness, unsanitary habits and that they willfully spread communicable diseases, including smallpox, among white centers. Such allegations were ridiculous.

In January, 1909, La Clerc openly circulated a petition to Congress asking that the Kalispel be removed from their lands in the Pend Oreille Valley. The circular alleged the Kalispel were nothing more than squatters on lands they did not own. Removal to the Coeur d' Alene Reservation was touted as the most humane treatment of the tribe for they did not have adequate housing, a church or school where they were now. The Indians were promised payment for any improvements made to the lands they would leave, "where they have been industrious enough to make any." Oddly, no provision was made to pay for the abandoned lands, only the improvements.

Perhaps it was because the Kalispel retained their cultural identity that they were a target of certain whites. The Kalispel were different from reservation Indians not only because they had no fixed boundaries, but also because they had not been schooled in, much less espoused, the white man's way. Digging camas, fishing and hunting, the Kalispel kept the ceremonies and traditional ways of life that faithfully preserved the integrity of their culture. Unfortunately, the tribe's fiscal stability was as ancient as their culture. Economically the Kalispel were pitiably destitute.

Captain Webster, for all his responsibilities to other tribes, stayed very close to the Kalispel situation. At his urging the tribe initiated a series of petitions to the federal government that finally brought results. Clair Hunt was appointed Special Alloting Agent for the Kalispel and instructed to place the Indians on their lands.

Agent Hunt was not especially sympathetic to the Kalispel cause at first. It was his incorrect impression that these Indians were a troublesome tribe who had never seriously resided in the Pend Oreille Valley until 1885, or about the same time the whites entered the region. When quizzed by Spokane reporters as to why the government was at last responding to a situation ripe for more than fifteen years, Hunt replied that "The government is providing them with lands in the valley where they have lived so long, in order that no idle class may be thrown on the white population." Later, upon investigating the Kalispel case more closely, Hunt came to respect the tribe for their forebearance in dealing with encroaching whites. He also found it remarkable the tribe lived in the old ways with absolutely no government aid, advice or administration. In the end, Hunt made allotments averaging forty acres apiece to the Kalispel and placed in his report the opinion that "the entire Pend Oreille Valley is land to which the Indian title had never been extinguished, and the Kalispel tribe has a moral right to recompense for the land taken by the whites."

In Washington D. C., the Hunt allotments failed to find approval in the Indian Bureau, once again leaving the Kalispel legally homeless. Hunt, it seems, found the Kalispel of 1909 on different sections than Bubb had placed them in his 1895 survey. The explanation was that individual Kalispel retained claim to certain lands, but financially pressed, rented these acres to whites, confining themselves to a village lot. The Bureau of Indian Affairs failed to comprehend the reasons for a switch and failed to formalize the Kalispel allotments. Anxious letters by the Kalispel and their agent went unanswered.

It is possible that this bizarre tale of government neglect might have ended in 1910 with the Kalispel diminishing in number, economically destitute and squatting on the public domain had it not been for Masselow. Blind and feeble at eighty-five years, the son of Victor knew the government had forgotten his tribe, but he could not perceive why the Jesuit fathers avoided his village. Since the days of De Smet and Hoecken the tribe had been solidly and devoutly Catholic. Then St. Ignatius Mission was moved to Montana, and only infrequently did a priest come to the Kalispel camps. Now it was twenty-five years since Mass had been said in Masselow's village. Determining to represent his tribe in one final grievance, Masselow left the Pend Oreille Valley headed for Gonzaga College.

Arriving at the college in Spokane after a journey of some sixty miles, Masselow, leaning on the arm of a companion, presented himself to the Jesuit President, Father Louis Taelman. He begged the priest to come to his people. In years past, he said, they annually went to Sacred Heart Mission on the Coeur d' Alene Reservation for the Corpus Christi feast. Now, intoned the chief, "Some of us are too weak, too old and sick to come to our fathers, and we come to ask you, Father Taelman, to come to us." Touched, the priest promised his personal visit on the Monday following.

Taelman was no ordinary priest and Masselow

FATHER LOUIS TAELMAN, S. J., Belgian-born Jesuit, was President of Gonzaga College in 1911 when he took up the Kalispel cause with a religious zeal. The youngish looking priest was prematurely dismissed from his post in 1913, after only four years, primarily because college affairs took second place to Kalispel needs.

knew it. For years Taelman had been a missionary on the Flathead Reservation, acquiring a rich knowledge of Salish Indians and, at the same time, becoming fluent in the Flathead and Kalispel language. The Jesuits had not neglected the Kalispel intentionally, it was only that the Kalispel, almost to a man, did not speak English, and therefore, few priests were capable of serving them. Taelman was one of only two or three persons who could converse in Kalispel.

The pilgrimage to the Indian camp on the Pend Oreille River was a human interest story not overlooked by Spokane newspapers. After all, the original impetus for sending Jesuits like Father De Smet to the Northwest had come when a group of Nez Perce walked to St. Louis in 1839, appeared on the steps of its great university, and appealed for a clergyman. The similarity of events was too great to resist. Father Taelman's subsequent trips to the village opposite Usk were widely reported and feature stories traced the history of the tribe, now measuring but 100 souls. For the first time in their history the Kalispel had publicity. In the capable hands of Taelman they would make the most of it.

As a priest Taelman served well the spiritual needs of the Kalispel. Children were baptized, marriages formalized, instructions given and Mass read on Church holidays. Commuting from Spokane was made more difficult by the remoteness of the tribe. Roads were poor and indirect, and there was not even a bridge across the river at Usk or Cusick.

Capitalizing on publicity for the tribe, Taelman launched a campaign to bring education to the Indian children. Investigations revealed that in the history of the tribe, no Kalispel had ever attended school. In addition, not a single tribesman could speak understandable English. At Taelman's insistence the Washington State delegation to Congress promised to seek funds for an Indian school, but while many news conferences were held, no building was actually funded. One of the highest hurdles to surpass was public opinion. The people of Spokane were reluctant to approve efforts by their Congressmen on behalf of the Kalispel because they judged all Indians by the shiftless ones then in the city. Taelman insisted the best way to make the Indians industrious was through schools near their village. There were in 1912 about twenty children, one-fifth of the tribe, growing up in ignorance. That same year Masselow voluntarily retired as chief and with tears in his sightless eyes begged Taelman to renew his quest for Indian schools.

All of the notoriety generated by Taelman's visits to the primitive tribe plus the agitation for a village school produced results. Congressman W. La Follette, in whose district the Kalispel village lay, entered an ammendment to the 1913

79

Indian Bill then in Congress providing for a federally funded school in Spokane for the Kalispel, and, more importantly, the setting aside of the 4,449 acres on which the tribe was then squatting. La Follette's ammendment was disallowed on a technicality, but the merit of the proposal was seen by others. With a minimum of delay, on March 24, 1914, President Woodrow Wilson by Executive Order set aside 4,629 acres of land on the east side of the Pend Oreille River as the Kalispel Indian Reservation.

The reservation opposite Usk and Cusick, so long fought for, was eight and one-half miles long and averaged one mile in width. It was barely one-thousandth of the acreage the Kalispel had called their own in aboriginal times! The tribe too was but a fraction of its former self being approximately one-tenth of the Kalispel population as first viewed by David Thompson. Still, it was a triumph.

THE TWENTIETH
CENTURY RESERVATION

In 1914 a flurry of activity produced not only a reservation, but also a new Catholic Church, Our Lady of Sorrows Indian Mission. Under the direction of Father Edward Griva, S.J., the tribesmen dedicated themselves to raising money and procuring building supplies. When finally completed, largely with Indian labor, the church became the social center of the reservation and is to this day a strong influence in the lives of the Kalispel. A government-sponsored school was also located on the reservation in 1913 and twenty-three young Kalispel studied academic and industrial skills. Adult education was also inaugurated, the most successful course being one on infant care.

The tribe fairly reeled under their acquisitions, only to learn the hard fact that nothing they had received thus far was lifting a sagging economy. Rushed into a world of the *Titanic,* World War I and Babe Ruth, the Kalispel were without means to either support themselves on the reservation or find sustenance off it. They learned what other tribes had known for decades before them: a reservation is no guarantee of future success.

The decade of the 1920's may have been glamorous and prosperous for many Americans, but not for the Kalispel. An unusually adaptable tribe if they wished to be, the Kalispel tried to learn the skills of the white man's way. Symbolically, Masselow, the retired chief and son of Victor, redoubtable figure of the old Kalispel ways, died in 1920 to the sorrow of his people. Chief John Bigsmoke endeavored to lead his tribe to economic stability but the effort floundered. The men were not farmers at heart and soon settled into the practice of leasing their lands to whites.

One of the few occupations to offer good pay was cougar hunting. The bounty on cougar was $35 and the pelt could be sold for up to $20, but few men were shrewd enough hunters to take this dangerous prey. Basil Andrews became a legend among the Kalispel for his solo exploits in the mountains, and also for his generosity in sharing the spoils of the hunt. How many big cats Basil killed is not known, but his proficiency was so great that newspapers at one time printed a running count.

The tribe was considerably more successful in matters concerning the law. In one case the Kalispel's agent, located among the Coeur d' Alenes, forbade gambling and "sporting" in the "Wild Oats" game at the tribe's annual pow wow. A pow wow is a great social and ceremonial occasion among the Northwest tribes and to curb this August affair was tantamount to a declaration of war to the Kalispel. Their response was not violent, however, but legal. An injunction was sought in federal court to restrain the order on grounds that the agent was outside the State of Washington. That the Kalispel lost the point of law is not as important as that they saw the law as a useful tool.

The most significant attempt by the Kalispels to make the law work in their favor was in 1927 when they engaged a Spokane attorney to carry to Congress a bill permitting the Kalispel to enter suit against the federal government in

Photograph Courtesy Alice Ignace

TAKEN ABOUT 1902, this photograph shows the Bigsmoke family's summer camp near the Pend Oreille River, Of interest are the bottom of the Kalispel canoe, the tipi pole framework, the manufactured clothing worn by everyone except the infant, Lucy on her Kalispel cradleboard. Future tribal chief John Bigsmoke stands on the left; holding the gun is Baptiste Bigsmoke, later the last chief of the Kalispel; Josephene, and Lucy on the cradleboard held by Susan Bigsmoke.

United States Claims Court for compensation at the rate of $1.25 an acre for all traditional lands confiscated without their permission. Chief Baptiste Bigsmoke, son of John Bigsmoke who passed away in 1926, argued a claim of one million dollars. The Kalispel bill did not pass.

The Depression Decade hit all Americans hard, but the Indian most of all. Already mired in abject poverty the Kalispels struggled to stay alive. Some New Deal legislation did find the tribe, most notably the Civilian Conservation Corps, which built some homes on the reservation, the Works Progress Administration, on whose projects a few Indians were employed, the Johnson-O'Malley Act, which provided for a new reservation education program, and the Indian Reorganization Act, which forced the tribe, in 1938, to charter itself under a new constitution as the Kalispel Indian Community.

For the next dozen years, until 1950, the Kalispel stagnated on the reservation. Little aided by the Bureau of Indian Affairs, save to formalize leases offered to Cusick cattlemen on the reservation bottomlands, the tribal government operated on a budget of less than $1,000 a year under a constitution that was unworkable by its town hall type of structure. Fewer than 100 Kalispel lived on the reservation, almost all in wretched, ill-vented houses that encouraged disease. Tribesmen submerged in a jobless economy were no longer uplifted by the natural

84

beauty of the region in which they lived, and the educational program, once so bright, was now defunct. Law enforcement with uncooperative state and county officers became another problem.

The Kalispel were suffering a deep culture shock. The aboriginal traditions, performed and perfected in so many generations, had been replaced in the twentieth century by acculturation. The social organization was altered, the religion modernized and the gathering economy supplanted by logging and laboring positions when possible.

THE INDIAN CLAIMS COMMISSION

The event that stirred the Kalispel to life was the 1946 legislation creating the Indian Claims Commission. Under its provisions the commission would hold hearings and make money settlements to remedy all frauds and injustices done to Indians by the federal government.

It was a neighboring tribe, the Upper Pend Oreilles, filing a claim with the "Confederated Salish and Kootenai Tribes" that brought to the Kalispel news of the Indian Claims Commission.

Learning of the Upper Pend Oreille claim in 1950 the Kalispel were at first miffed, then outraged. First of all, no one had asked the Kalispel to join in the claim, apparently overlooking their rich Salish heritage. Then, upon closer examination of the Upper Pend Oreille case, the Kalispels found that tribe claiming territory which both tribes had occupied jointly, plus some lands which the Kalispel regarded as exclusively their own. For once the unweildy Kalispel Indian Community government functioned advantageously as the entire tribe met to discuss the situation. Few in the tribe appreciated being left out of the Upper Pend Oreille action, yet almost none wanted to make a claim of their own. Those who did, notably Louis Andrews, Tribal Chairman, and Alice Ignace, the Secretary, were dedicated and hard workers. Research was begun in the Jesuits' Oregon Province Archives on the Gonzaga University campus in 1950 and that same year claims attorneys were hired on a contingency contract. The small number of tribesmen who held faith in the project persevered at great personal expense. The tribal secretary, for example, would have to solicit door to door donations on the reservation in order to attend meetings in Spokane.

In the next several years there was much hope, but a great deal more patience. The first witness for the Kalispel, a Jesuit priest by no small coincidence, testified in January of 1952. Due to unavoidable delays, the next petitioner's witness was not called for another two and one-half years! Four years after that, in June of 1958, the commission offered its opinion, finding that on or about the year 1890 the

Kalispel had been systematically denied use of their aboriginal property, then had their lands forcibly seized by the government who paid no consideration.

The tribe was soon to learn that securing the approval of the Indian Claims Commission was not the final step, only a first step in winning their case. It would not be until 1961, after further arguments, that the commission would arbitrarily fix the date of full government acquisition of the land as July 1, 1903. Two more years elapsed before the commission set damages to the Kalispel at three million dollars, less ten percent for attorney fees. The next step in the white man's system of justice was the appropriation of $2.7 million, done in 1963. One final requirement stood between the Kalispel and their money.

The 1964 Interior Department Appropriation Act stated that awards from the Indian Claims Commission could not be finalized until a report of the purposes for which the funds were to be used had been submitted and approved in Senate and House Interior Committees.

Meeting the tribal attorneys, Bureau of Indian Affairs Officials, the county agent and the Cusick elementary school principal, the tribe broke into committees to determine the needs of the tribe and to propose budgets. The dilapidated, abandoned school house on the reservation became the tribe's gathering point.

In winter the wood-burning stove was kept continuously fired to melt the snow on the roof to keep accumulations from collapsing the building. The entire tribe took an interest in the judgment fund program and even enrolled members living off the reservation came to sessions, sometimes swelling attendance to 116 persons. The program devised by the tribe in February of 1964 aimed for guided acculturation. Non-reservation members were considered as well as resident members, but in both cases the youth of the tribe received primary emphasis for it was they who would live in the complex world of tomorrow.

Almost simultaneously that same month Congressman Walt Horan and Senator Henry M. Jackson introduced into Congress similar bills providing for the disposition of the Kalispel judgment fund, previously appropriated and temporarily on deposit in the Treasury. The fourteen year delay seemed finally at an end when the House passed the bill and August 10 it was approved by the Senate. Only approval of the Commissioner of Indian Affairs was needed for the release of the judgment fund. Regretably, there were unseen difficulties.

Certainly the Kalispel's comprehensive judgment fund program was acceptable. In fact, it was a model of its kind, incorporating the best ideas of other tribe's plans while tailoring itself to the Kalispel's specific needs. The roadblock now was a "Committee Comment" attached to the bill by the Senate Committee on Interior and Insular Affairs, requiring a Bureau of Indian Affairs report on the practicality of placing the administration of the program under a private trustee. This committee, chaired by the Kalispel's own Senator Jackson from Washington, had previously been informed that such an idea was unworkable in the tribe's plan, though likely it would be applied to certain portions of the program such as the youth scholarship, recreation and education monies. The "Committee Comment" further expressed concern about the failure of the Bureau of Indian Affairs to carry out past legislation relating to termination programs for tribes and stated "It is the sense of the committee, in view of the size of this judgment and the plan for the use of the money, that the Kalispel Tribe should be moved toward termination of Federal supervision."

After a tedious year of waiting, the Bureau of Indian Affairs furnished the Senate Interior Committee with the requested report regarding a private trustee for the Kalispel judgment program. No fault was found by them in the tribe's original presentation. When the committee did not accept that report the tribe knew the private trustee question was not the real issue. The Jackson committee, it seemed, was willing to release the $2.7 million fund only if the tribe agreed to termination. Stoicly, the tribe that had refused government ultimatums in decades before, rejected them again. The tribe let it be known that they would rather lose their judgment than terminate.

The Coeur d' Alenes, Colvilles, Spokanes and other tribes represented formally by the Affiliated Tribes of Northwest Indians, stepped in to comfort the Kalispel. They passed resolutions and brought pressure to bear on Congress. They knew that the Kalispel, if anything, should be one of the last tribes terminated.

The Senate Interior Committee shrank under the publicity. On the record the tribe had won a claims judgment, the money was appropriated, the bill for use of the fund was passed and the Bureau of Indian Affairs approved the tribe's fund program. Only a Senate committee refused to set the money free, attempting to create legislation that would effectively nullify the judgment bill. Shortly, the objections of the committee were removed and in October, 1965, the Kalispel at last had permission to proceed in its tribal-wide program.

Placing the judgment fund program into effect was a pleasurable moment for the Kalispel. Fifty percent of the judgment was invested, mostly in United States Treasury bonds, while the other half was to be allocated to the tribe's immediate and near future needs. Of pressing concern was the implementation of

90

Photograph by Thomas A. Carriker

CALISPELL PEAK (6,837 feet) daily casts its shadow on the Kalispel People. Since aboriginal times, this mountain has been a landmark for inhabitants and travelers in the Pend Oreille Valley.

the Family Plan whereby $7,000 was available to each enrollee. All of the parents' portions and up to $2,500 of each child's portion were available for buying a house. In 1965 there were twenty-one ramshackle, wood-frame houses on the reservation, seventeen of which were shared by more than one family. One year later eleven homes were under plans and nineteen new homes were already built on the reservation with indoor plumbing, electricity, running water and adequate living space. Another nineteen homes were partially funded for enrolled members living outside the reservation.

The youth program, so important to the forward looking tribal council, included budgeted funds for scholarships, grants, planned recreation plus a trust fund for each youth under eighteen. When finally completed, the trust fund amounted to $447,000 for eighty-two children.

Not the least important program funded by the claims commission judgment was the large amount set aside for investment in Indian employment enterprises, purchase of new lands, and the building of a community building. The Community Center was the first of these projects to see realization when $75,000 was earmarked for its construction. Inexperienced in fiscal matters, the tribe was unaware until the building was almost dedicated in December of 1967 that federal grants were available for up to

$44,000 of the building's cost.

These were learning years. A poor and unlettered tribe since the turn of the century, the Kalispel were suddenly thrust into a world of high finance. Only one tribesman had even completed high school. Under the circumstances, properly managed tribal funds were accomplished through a combination of study, reliance upon the tribal attorney and consultation with the Bureau of Indian Affairs' officers in whom the tribe had confidence.

Money did not solve all the Kalispel problems as the year following the granting of funds showed. Proud new homeowners, for example, were inexperienced in maintenance skills. Fully thirty percent of the tribe was under medication for tuberculosis. Students failed to take advantage of scholarship offerings, lacking a tradition to complete their education or even to take it seriously. An interpreter was still needed at tribal meetings, and, worst of all, no new jobs opened up in the immediate vicinity. In fact, in 1966 only one Kalispel male living on the reservation was gainfully employed. The tribe was almost wholly dependent on welfare for its survival.

A new problem facing the Kalispel in the mid-1960's was the status of land allotments. As part of the New Deal legislation the Kalispel had been alloted individual plots on the reservation. For the next thirty years the tribe made no declaration of which legal allotment belonged to which tribesman, for all who occupied the reservation considered it common land. The newly endowed tribal government, attempting to find suitable sites to invite job producing businesses, suddenly became acutely conscious of what land belonged to whom. A tracing of records discovered that the tribe owned 150 acres of land in common and there were, in addition, 107 individual allotments varying in size from 70.8 acres to 33.95 acres. These allotments were owned by only ninety persons, some of whom could not be located. In addition to the reservation allotments there were six allotments totaling 216 acres on the west bank of the Pend Oreille River. This property had been leased by the Bureau of Indian Affairs in 1962 to a lumber company. Other allotments were under lease too. A total of 936 acres in thirty-four sections, was given over to nearby ranchers.

By 1967 the tribe had ironed out some of its difficulties and was making progress. For one thing the 1938 constitution was scrapped in favor of a more efficient, liberal and business-like charter, including the eighteen year old vote. The new Community Building provided office space, meeting rooms and recreational facilities. The tribe, further, became conscious of national and regional Indian affairs and began to participate in intertribal associations. The

94

Photograph by Charles A. Steen, Jr.

OUR LADY OF SORROWS ROMAN CATHOLIC MISSION to the Kalispel people, the only church on the reservation, was built in 1914 with Indian labor. Services are still held in this mission in 1973.

Land Purchase Program of the tribe was also inaugurated in that year.

Just as the Kalispel seemed confident of their ability to manage their own affairs the dark cloud of termination re-appeared. As a shock to nearly all the Northwest tribes, let alone the Kalispel, Senator Henry Jackson's Interior Committee in 1967 requested the Commissioner of Indian Affairs to draft legislation terminating four Oklahoma tribes and the Kalispel. No one could understand the Kalispel's selection.

Resentfully, the Kalispel fought the termination attempt. They would not lightly lose their property trust status, the supervision of the Indian Bureau plus the supportive services. Congressman Tom Foley's aid was enlisted and he pledged full support, acknowledging no termination bill could pass Congress with tribal opposition. Yet, the tribe knew, if the bill were entered they would have to bear the burden and expense of fighting passage. Petitions and resolutions were offered to show the tribe was one-hundred percent against termination.

In the end Senator Jackson cancelled his plans to enter terminal legislation for the Kalispel. Unofficially the Kalispel were told they had never really been threatened, for the real reason the Senate Interior Committee had begun the action was merely to scare the Indian Bureau into a favorable response to a number of requests from the committee regarding some judgment cases. The legislation may have been pretend, but the panic of the Kalispel was not.

Returning to normal, the tribe resumed its affairs. One of the major items in the Kalispel budget has been the Land Purchase Program whereby $100,000 was made available to buy land adjoining or across from the reservation. Fairly surrounded by the Kaniksu National Forest and the small towns of Usk and Cusick there was, unfortunately, little opportunity to buy new lands from whites. Interestingly, it was the reverse situation which stimulated the tribe's land purchase committee. Land purchase funds could also be used to acquire Kalispel members' allotments. When one tribesman sold his forty acre allotment to a white man, the shocked tribal council resolved not to let it happen again. They then began to secure the reservation's Indian integrity by buying all available allotments. By the close of 1970 the tribe had bought twenty-four allotments for over $98,000 and received another $50,000 from the tribe's budget to purchase another dozen tracts.

By the beginning of the decade of the 1970's the Kalispel had come of age. The educational level of the tribe had been raised, partly because the tribe was working closely with the Cusick school system. As proof of their success the tribe pointed to a Ford Foundation Leadership Grant won by one of its young men. Yet, there was the persistent problem of employment.

Only 3.5% of the tribe was fully employed, 19.5% were underemployed and 77% were unemployed. The median family income was deplorably low at $2,600 yearly.

Securing Indian jobs in the Pend Oreille Valley was never easy. The region itself is static economically and Indians have never been favored employees. One of the objectives of the judgment fund was to encourage new business to the area, but that was not easy. Things became worse when the lumber company leasing the tribal land burned down and did not rebuild. The tribe was approached on several deals. Finally, in 1971, the tribe made its first major investment by placing funds in an Aluminum Box plant at Cusick.

One source of jobs located by the tribe has been government programs. Through persistence and ingenuity the Kalispel have placed up to ten men on certain federal and state funded projects. From 1967 through 1971, for example, the tribe received grants to pay for Indian crews laboring on building, roofing and painting details in nearby white communities like Newport and Cusick. In 1973 the Washington State Economic Assistance Authority awarded the Kalispel a loan of $300,000 for development of an industrial park on tribal lands across from the reservation, but it is temporarily in dispute before the Washington State Supreme Court. The tribe fully realizes such programs are tem-

98

Photograph by Robert D. Dellwo

CREW OF TRIBAL WORK EXPERIENCE MEN preparing to set out to work. This photograph by the Kalispel tribal attorney shows the forest environment of the Kalispel people today.

porary and that long-term employment must be found.

THE FUTURE

The future looks bright for the Kalispel. Traditionally a close-knit tribe, the family spirit envelops the reservation today. Of the 160 enrolled members of the tribe about 100 live on the reservation and another thirty live within 100 miles. The threat of termination is now history and the tribe is content living in the beautiful Pend Oreille Valley.

Though many tribes, such as the neighboring Colvilles, are experiencing a division of their tribe among those who will not leave the reservation and those who prefer the city, the Kalispel have no such struggle. There is much to be desired in terms of on reservation health care, for the tribe's nearest hospital is Newport and dental care is offered only in Spokane, but steps are being taken to remedy these problems.

Jobs continue to be the most persistent problem of the Kalispel. The Aluminum Box factory, a non-polluting industry producing tool boxes, laundry carts and camper-tops for pickup trucks has not proved worthy of the tribe's $90,000 investment, but it is yet too early to make a final statement. It is anticipated that in the future the tribe will branch into the live-stock areas, gradually calling in leases to make the grassland available to tribal owned stock.

100

The greatest hope for the future lies in the industrial site on the west bank of the Pend Oreille River. Served by a railroad, highway and water this could be a real asset in the future.

Recreational possibilities are also being considered by the tribe. Holding eight miles of riverfront on the broad, lake-like Pend Oreille River, the tribe could easily develop a major resort area. The region is already a favorite of vacationers from Southern California. To do this, however, the advantage of secluded reservation life, say many in the tribe, would be destroyed. Thus far no firm commitment has been made, partly because an additional drawback to such a proposition is that the tribe would have to acquire ownership to vast stretches of allotted lands and not all tribesmen will sell. By the same token, the Manresa Grotto, because of its historic importance and legendary significance, could be a tourist attraction, but the caves and a lagoon adjacent are part of allotment 104 whose heirs cannot be located.

The Kalispel's interest in their young people is almost fanatical. The claims commission judgment provided a substantial trust fund for each enrolled child and it is the hope of the tribe that useful trades and skills will result from the concurrent maturing of both the children and their funds. In the interim, a new Youth Center, presently under construction adjacent to the church, will mold and develop their ambitions.

101

Neglected by the federal government, various churchmen and the general public for so many decades, the Kalispel have also been overlooked by the scholarly community. There are neither books on the Kalispel as a tribe, nor journal articles dealing with them. Books and articles that deal with the tribe even peripherally are rare. The present book is, in fact, the first publication on the Kalispel people.

CHITTENDEN, H. M. AND A. T. RICHARDSON. *Life, Letters and Travel of Father Pierre-Jean De Smet, S.J.,* New York: Harper, 1905. 4 Vols.

Inasmuch as De Smet wrote letters in French, Flemish, Dutch, German and Italian, we are fortunate to have this popular translation.

CURTIS, EDWARD S. *The North American Indian.* Vol. VII. Norwood, Mass.: Plimpton Press, 1911.

DAVIS, WILLIAM L., S.J., *A History of St. Ignatius Mission.* Spokane: C. W. Hill, 1954.

Brief but incisive treatment of the ten year tenure of the mission on the Pend Oreille River before it was moved to Montana.

DE SMET, PIERRE-JEAN, S. J., *Letters and Sketches: With a Narrative of a Year's Residence Among the Indian Tribes of the Rocky Mountains, 1845-46.* New York: Edward Dunigan, 1847.

Rare book, but worth the effort to locate.

DIOMEDI, ALEXANDER, S.J., *Sketches of Modern Indian Life.* Woodstock: Woodstock Press, 1884.

A rare book, but one of the few sources available on the Kalispels and Coeur d' Alenes in the period 1868-1878.

GARRAGHAN, GILBERT J., *S.J., The Jesuits of the Middle United States.* 3 Vols. New York: American Press, 1938.

Volume II reports the Jesuit interest in the Pacific Northwest, with references to the Kalispel and St. Ignatius Mission.

RAY, VERNE F. "Cultural Relations in the Plateau of Northwestern America," *Publications of the Frederick Webb Hodge Anniversity Publication Board,* Vol. III. Los Angeles: Southwest Museum, 1939.

Includes the Interior Salish tribes.

ROBERT C. CARRIKER is an Associate Professor of History at Gonzaga University, Spokane, Washington. A native of Missouri, Carriker received his B.S. from Saint Louis University and a Ph.D. from neighboring University of Oklahoma. Carriker is the author of two other books dealing with Western Indian and military affairs, the recipient of two Henry E. Huntington Library grants and a veteran of the American Indian Research Project of oral history on the Kalispel Reservation. During 1972 Dr. Carriker was Visiting Lecturer in American Indian History at Arizona State University.

One area of interest important to old and young alike is the history of their tribe. School-age children want to learn more about the old customs, the old stories and the character of the great chiefs. Before long it is hoped Kalispel Indian history will be taught on the reservation and in the local schools. When the full record of the Kalispel people is brought forth the pride of the tribe may properly blossom out.